A Letter To My Sisters

Voncele Savage

Savage House
Canton, Mississippi

Dedication

To my son Ty, and my daughter April.
You endured. You survived. I love you dearly.

And the Spirit and the bride say, Come.
And let him that heareth say, Come.
And let him that is athirst come.
And whosoever will, let him take the water of life freely.

Revelation 22:17

Acknowledgments

My first acknowledgment is to my Lord and Savior Jesus Christ, who saved me, raised me and put a longing in my spirit to console my many sisters within the church, that have withstood the many adversities and vicissitudes that life has thrust upon them.

My humble thanks is extended to Natasha Moore for her unselfish wit, wisdom and knowledge that she patiently gave as she acted as midwife for the birth of this book.

To all my prayer-partners and friends who tolerated me while I awkwardly endeavored to complete this task, I breath a hardy thank you.

A special thank you to Dr. Walter Williams, Pastor of Antioch M.B. Church, Yazoo City, Mississippi. Because of his faithfulness to his calling, he has encouraged me and given me a listening ear when needed.

Table Of Contents

Key Scriptures

And they shall be mine, saith the Lord of hosts, in that day when I make up my jewels, and I will spare them, as a man spareth his own son that serveth him. (Malachi 3:17)

"They will be mine," says the Lord Almighty, "in the day when I make up my treasured possession. I will spare them, just as in compassion a man spares his son who serves him."(Malachi 3:17 The New International Version)

Purpose

To inspire with courage, spirit, or hope; to encourage, to highlight and bring to the forefront; to awaken; to enlighten; to instruct; to give insight to (Webster's Dictionary)

A box holds in place, protects, and keeps secure. It keeps the contents from destruction. It can cushion and cover up so that what is inside will not be lost or destroyed. It can keep the contents from being revealed or exposed before the proper time. This can be desirable or undesirable, depending on the contents. It also protects from the outside environment. If properly constructed, nothing that does not belong inside the box can get in. This can pertain to anything that can be harmful.

I want my sisters to be aware of the fact that when we are in Christ, He keeps us under the blood. We are protected and preserved until He returns. We are placed into His jewelry box where he protects and preserves us for eternity. While we are in the box, he prepares us for emerging from the box.

Preface

I greet my sisters in the name of the Lord Jesus Christ. It is needful that the truth is told at this time. The truth will make you free. "The righteous cry, and the Lord heareth, and delivereth them out of all their troubles." (Psalms 34:17) That is a continuous process, not just a one-time event. "Blessed be the Lord, who daily loadeth us with benefits" (Psalms 68:19a)

This book was not written as an expose, a tell everything, or to spew out bitterness. It is a healing agent. It was written to fill a void, to fulfill a need for my sisters, and to let you know you are not alone. You are not isolated. There are others that have been, or are currently in the same situation.

I used to watch television and look disdainfully upon those that were open and revealing with their personal lives. I would say with a smirk, that everybody is writing a book, or "telling it all". I did not see that some people simply have a passion for life, and those that are on that path with them. At some point in your life, you must come to the realization that you cannot just sit passively by and not contribute or be a factor in the lives of those with whom you share a destiny.

There are so many wounded, hurting sisters sitting quietly in our churches, and smothering who they really are. They exist in quiet desperation. I have had some say to me, "Your testimony was very encouraging to me. I'm glad to know someone else is going through the same thing I am, and that I am not alone." They were just waiting for some-one to speak out. These women have become my passion. There have been occasions when I was talking to someone, not realizing that a sister with a listening ear was nearby, re-ceiving strength from my conversation, and I was informed later that she had received encouragement from what she heard me say. That is why it is so important to walk in the Spirit and not be carnal. A philosopher once said, "Yours is not to reason why. Yours is to do or die."

We are to yield our members to God twenty-four hours a day, seven days a week. It is vital that the saints of God are there for each other. We must be sensitive to the needs of the other parts of the body of Christ. If one part of the body is weak or infected, it affects the rest of the body. A chain is no stronger than its weakest link. We are to stand together against the forces of evil.

This is not a book about a man. It is about the deception of the enemy. The devil has deceived so many women into thinking they must suffer abuse in silence. His most obvi-ous strategy is to divide and conquer. He has told them there is no way out, so therefore, if we do not communi-cate with each other, he can work his cunning tactics with-out any resistance.

In this book, I am confronting those things that would come against my sisters in the body of Christ in order to block their progress in the spiritual realm, thereby hinder-ing them in every aspect of their daily life. I am particularly addressing the issue of abuse and ungodly relationships with the opposite gender.

The adversary has even distorted the definition of abuse. Please be aware that abuse comes in different forms. Abuse takes place when something or someone is used for a purpose other than for what he, she, or it was designed or created. There is emotional, mental, verbal, sexual, as well as physical abuse.

Because so much energy is used in surviving amidst turmoil when someone is in an abusive relationship, the body of Christ suffers, because the abused person becomes unproductive and no longer bears fruit. By being unfruitful, there is no growth. We become stagnant. This can lead to death, spiritually and naturally. Remember, our Lord cursed the fig tree because it was not producing. It was unfruitful and not doing what it was created to do, and that was to bear fruit. Christ came to give us life, and that more abundantly.

It is my prayer that someone will be liberated by reading this book and walk in the gifts and anointing of the Holy Ghost. I pray that the words in this book usher healing into your spirit as the Word of God will validate them. I pray that it will help you find direction. It is written from the perspective of one who has found THE WAY OUT.

This book began to be formed in my spirit around 2003, but because I was not ready spiritually, I could not fulfill that vision. I had to lay myself on the altar first, and let the Lord heal me from the inside to the outside. I had too much anger, hurt and bitterness within me. All I could do at that time was to regurgitate and spew out poison that would have contaminated and defiled instead of enlightening and encouraging. For this reason, I was stymied from all human efforts regarding writing.

God loves me so much, that He put me in a quiet place, away from a lot of distraction and things that would divert me from the path I was to follow in order to find THE WAY OUT.

AT VARIOUS POINTS THROUGHOUT THIS BOOK, I HAVE LEFT ROOM FOR PERSONAL NOTES IN ORDER TO HELP YOU CLARIFY AND ILLUMINATE YOUR THOUGHTS.

NOTES

_____

_____

_____

_____

_____

Introduction

It seems that too many of us do not have a vision. We do not have a purpose. We do not have foresight or any enthusiasm about what is in the future.

Sometimes it seems as though we wander aimlessly through life, with no definite goals in mind. When you do not have a vision, you do not have hope. Hope makes us alive. It gives us purpose. Without hope or a vision, we become zombies. We just roll with the punches and take whatever life puts on our plate. Most of the time, we do not realize what is happening to us. We become acclimated to the conditions in which we exist. We go from day to day, numb, cold, and without feeling. This is not what God intended. Acts 1:8 tells us we shall have power after the Holy Ghost is come upon us.

We know all the correct procedures and how to go through the drill, so to speak. Others see what they think is a functioning, living profile that is saying and doing the right things at the right time. Actually, it is just an outline or representation of what is perceived to be real. They do not realize they are looking at a mere shadow or vague image. This can be so deceiving. We have learned to be great pretenders. It is not that we intentionally practice deception in order to hurt others, but we do it to protect ourselves. We think we can keep our sanity by acting like a little girl playing house. Many times, it is a ploy we use to keep the proverbial wolf away from our door.

There are so many women sitting on our church pews with secrets covered up with false faces, big hats and beautiful clothes. Inside them, there is pain, insecurity, doubt, confusion and fear. We have learned how to look, how to walk, and how to talk. The outward personification can be very misleading. Our churches on Sunday mornings and other meeting times have become stages and we are the actors. "Praise the Lord Sister Tomato. How are you?" "I'm blessed and highly favored." It seems that sometimes we are simply playing the childhood game of charades by acting out our lives in front of amused bystanders. The old cliché says we can fool some of the people some of the time but you and I both know we cannot fool God at any time.

It is time for us to rewrite the script. Take off the false face and reveal your real character. Come out of the fog. Look life squarely in the face and walk in the victory we have in Christ Jesus. Come out from behind the façade.

I used to be very good at playing my part of a good mother, obedient wife, well-prepared professional (teacher) and a contributing member of society. In fact, I became lost in those identities. I was able to adapt to my circumstances and became numb to my true emotions and feelings. There were times when I did not know from one minute to the next, what I was going to do. I dared not make too many plans. I had become resigned to the fact that my plans and dreams were of no consequence to my spouse. I catered to what he wanted, and he made it perfectly clear he was not interested in what I wanted.

When you find THE WAY OUT, you will know that you do not have to go through "the drill" as the saying goes. You can live in "real time" and be yourself, without fear of condemnation and rejection. "Stand fast therefore in the liberty wherewith Christ hath made us free, and be not entangled again with the yoke of bondage." (Galatians 5:1) When you repent, and are baptized in Jesus' name and receive the Holy Ghost, you do not have to be in bondage to the obstacles that satan sets before you.

No marriage should rob either spouse of his/her individuality, or uniqueness. It is uniqueness that makes each one different or worthy of note. When you lose your special characteristics that make up your personality, you become "wallpaper", so to speak. You are just decoration for that setting. Your uniqueness should complement each other, not disparage or obliterate each other.

When you know who you are in Christ, you can achieve the type of relationships God has ordained for you, because "He hath made us accepted in the beloved." (Ephesians 1:6a)

God's Jewels

You belong to Jesus. God gave you to Him. He paid an immeasurable price. He redeemed (paid for) you with His blood. He keeps you in a special place when you develop a relationship with Him and accept Him as your Savior. As the natural daddy is with his son, so is God with His children.

You know how some parents sometimes have a favorite child. It is not that they love that child any more than they love the other(s), but it is usually because that child is more obedient and causes the least trouble that the parent tends to grant or give more favor. The parent knows they can trust that child.

We know God is no respecter of person, but all of His promises are conditional. When we make the effort or commitment to do the things that are pleasing to Him, He rewards us with His abundant blessings. Some benefits we receive as children of God just because He loves us, but others are like a bonus. We receive them because we seek after Him and are obedient to

His Word. He grants special favor to those who "diligently seek Him" (Hebrews 11:6). The Word says He rewards us.

Our heavenly Father has pity or compassion on us when we turn to Him. Consider Matthew 15:20, 24, where we find the story of the prodigal son. God never rejects us. It is not in His nature to do so. God is love. He patiently waits for circumstances and situations to lead us back to Him, and He is standing there with outstretched arms to receive us. He will welcome us into His Kingdom and load many gifts upon us.

God wrapped himself in flesh and died for us. His love is past all understanding. Our human vocabulary cannot fully describe His unfathomable, profound, love that daily shows us grace and mercy.

Follow Jesus and He will heal you. He will make you whole. Matthew 12: 15 and 19:2 are examples of how He heals those who follow Him. If you follow, that is become a disciple or student of the Word (Jesus), you will be healed when you discipline or train your life according to the written and spoken Word and you consume the Word and internalize it. The essential thing is to believe. "Faith is the substance of things hoped for, the evidence of things not seen." (Hebrews 11: l) Life becomes reality based upon your faith. I once heard my daughter say, "Your perception is your reality." For some reason, that stuck in my spirit. What do you perceive for your life's meaning and function? Do you see yourself as God sees you?

"He sent His Word and healed them, and delivered them from their destructions." (Psalms 109:20). Also consider,

2

"But unto you that fear my name shall the Sun of righteousness arise with healing in His wings." (Malachi 2:4a) We know that God can take the heat out of the fire even as you walk amidst the flames. He did it for the Hebrew boys: Shadrach, Meshach and Abednego. I am not addressing salvation specifically. I am more explicitly dealing with the issue of our walk of faith.

After you are saved, then what happens? Do you have direction? Christians receive their marching orders from the Word of God. The written Word is our road map through life.

When you are in emotional and mental pain, you are in distress and in bondage to something that is contrary to the Word of God. When we are allowing the Word to abide in us and we abide in the Word, we find peace and contentment.

We sometimes become so consumed by what is happening in our lives that we fail to seek direction from God. We must pray and seek counsel from God and then after we pray, we must wait for an answer. I know this is the microwave generation, but God is not an instant genie in a bottle.

I used to sit on my living room sofa, numb, and just waiting for things to change without even talking to my heavenly father about what was going on in my life. I would just sit there and wait for the next attack, going through my daily routine by remote. I had mentally and emotionally separated myself from my surroundings. I had virtually shut down emotionally and mentally.

"In all thy ways acknowledge Him, and He shall direct thy paths." (Proverbs 3:6) In order to acknowledge Him, you have to recognize His presence. You have to know that He is eternally present (omnipresent). He is always available for us to ask, seek and knock.

"Let us therefore come boldly unto the throne of grace, that we may obtain mercy and find grace to help in time of need." (Hebrews 4:16) Praying is an act of faith. It is a participatory activity. It is not a vague phenomenon. Prayer is an experience that links us to the ultimate power, and that power is God. He is our source.

There were times when I tried to defy the enemy by becoming quiet and unobtrusive, instead of praying. We must fight with our God-given spiritual equipment. "Submit yourselves therefore to God. Resist the devil, and he will flee from you." (James 4:7) Use your kingdom power. You are not a helpless victim. You are a victor in Christ Jesus. Do not resort to the tactics of the enemy. "I will lift up mine eyes unto the hills, from whence cometh my help. My help cometh from the Lord, which made heaven and earth." (Psalms 121:1-2)

I am a diamond in the rough. You are a diamond in the rough. We are God's jewels. We are His treasured possessions. We are highly valued. We are of extreme importance to Him. We are highly esteemed in the eyes of God. We are hidden in His jewelry box. We are in a special place, where He keeps His treasures. We are being shaped and molded into one of the most precious gemstones in the world. In fact, there is no gemstone in the world as precious as we are. According to the Random House Encyclopedia, the largest cut diamond in the world is the Star of Africa, weighing a little over 530 carets. It has no value when compared to how God values each soul that comes to Him.

If you want to be one of His jewels, he must prepare you. Diamonds are used as gems, abrasives or cutting tools. It takes time and a special period of preparation for each kind of jewel to be formed. We are God's peculiar treasure. Peculiar does not mean odd or weird. In the Hebrew language, it means special. (Strong's Exhaustive Concordance of the Bible). You are special. I am not implying that God puts you through pain and disappointment in order to punish you, as some religious people seem to think. I do know that He will use everything to His glory and for your benefit.

A treasure is something to be valued. It has great worth. It is not cast carelessly aside or thrown away intentionally. When you treasure something, you do your best to take good care of it and see that it is in the right environment. I know that sometimes we have inexpensive little trinkets that do not have much value, but that is not what we are to God. We are highly regarded.

A diamond is formed under pressure. The stronger the pressure applied, the more purity or clarity is produced. If you do not recognize what you are looking at you may throw it aside as a piece of coal, to be burned in the furnace. It is not evident at first, that it is something to be highly prized and valued. We are being conformed into the image of Christ (Romans 8:29). They did not recognize Him either. They hung Him on a cross. When we are made into the image of Christ, we cannot get any more pure than that. "For in Him dwells all the fullness of the Godhead bodily". (Colossians 12:9)

In the deep innermost recesses of the earth, you find diamonds sequestered, (tucked) away, waiting to be revealed. "For now we are looking in a mirror that gives only a dim reflection, but then we shall see in reality and face to face!" (1 Corinthians 13:12a) Consider the parallel. As diamonds are formed, the pressure keeps mounting, and so does the heat. When that diamond is dug out of the deep recesses of the earth, it may initially appear to be just another rock. In fact, I am sure you have heard the expression, "wow, what a rock." However, after it is brought to the earth's surface, it is given special care and treatment and prepared for the merchant or jeweler to put it on display for others to see.

No pain-no gain. No cross- no crown. "He that taketh not his cross, and follows after me, is not worthy of me." (Matthew 10:38). After the period of preparation, the true beauty is revealed. The key is to have enough of the Word in you to know when you are being shaped and molded into the image of Christ, or when you are following your own pernicious ways.

This does not mean we should suffer pain and disappointment in order to mature spiritually. However, it does mean we will mature as a result of suffering pain and disappointment. Think about it.

(Colossians 2:3)…. "In whom are hid all the treasures of wisdom and knowledge." When we are in Christ, we partake of the heavenly treasures of wisdom and knowledge.

We know which paths to follow and which decisions to make because the Lord orders our steps. Our trials truly do come to make us stronger. As we mature spiritually, we learn how to apply the Word to our life. We no longer are innocent bystanders. We control our environment. We do not let our environment control us. I once heard someone say we become the thermostat instead of the thermometer. The thermostat controls the environment, while the thermometer only reacts to the environment. Which one are you?

You may say, "God don't you see? Where are you?" Yes, He sees and He hears. He is in the midst of it all. Nothing just happens. Whether you initiated the action or allowed satan to initiate it, God is still in control. God may not have caused the circumstances, but He can work them for your good. "And we know that all things work together for good to them that love God, to them who are the called according to his purpose." (Romans 8:28) How do you think you arrived at this point in your life? It is because He brought you through the heat and the pressure. "He is the author and finisher of our faith." (Hebrews 12:2) That means Jesus is the leader or captain. He is in charge. He is the source and the resource. We originated in Him. He is our creator. He supplies our needs. He is the I Am, (as in I Am whatever you need me to be). He is the all-sufficient one. The power flows from Him. He is the generator. You are not guiding the ship, and you are not sailing blind if you are letting the Word be your compass.

When all the elements are in the right position and the season for being revealed comes, then God's special jewels will be revealed; but for now we see thru a glass darkly, but

I "am persuaded that He is able to keep that which I (we) have committed unto Him against that day." (2 Timothy 1:12b).

Your husband left you. You lost your job. Your son is in jail. Your daughter is a crack addict. Your neighbor lied on you. Your daddy touched you in a way he should not have. Your lights were turned off and you were evicted from your home. Your car was repossessed. The doctor said you have breast cancer. Your brother or cousin said, "Let's play house." Your husband is the perfect image of a brother in Christ in public, but the true character of a demon from hell behind closed doors. God can and will work through all of it if you allow Him. It takes time for a jewel to be formed. Trust God to complete His work.

DO NOT LAY THIS BOOK DOWN YET! I am not saying by any stretch of the imagination that we are to endure abuse of any kind. Read on and see how the Lord can work in your situation. Just kick back in the Holy Ghost and watch God work it out.

Zig Ziglar said, "Remember, it's not what happens to you; it's how you handle what happens to you that's going to make the difference in your life."

You are a diamond being formed for the master's jewelry box. When you come forth, you will shine with a brightness and clarity that will baffle the world's jewelers. You will be pure and unblemished. People looked at me and marveled how I survived. Some could not understand why I persisted in staying in such a dysfunctional marriage. At the time, I did not see it as being dysfunctional.

Just to bring some clarity into the equation, I must say that I did not realize where I was in relation to using the rest of society as my barometer. I felt that for all intensive purposes I was doing quite well. Others around me tried to stir me away from troubled waters, but I was intent upon navigating through the obstacles my way. The problem with that was I did not have life experiences or the wisdom to stay on course. I was floundering and did not know I was about to drown.

There were periods of time when my relationship with my husband was tolerable. I can even remember moments of happiness until something would happen to jerk me back into reality. The ecstasy never prevailed for long. Then I would ride that wave and move on until another gentle breeze would blow. There were times when I was lulled into thinking that things would get better. I wanted so much to believe that we could have a happy marriage and be a healthy family.

I do not delude myself into thinking that there are any perfect marriages, because I know we are imperfect beings. In spite of that fact, there are many sound marriages, rooted and grounded in Jesus Christ. Both partners have to make a committed effort to bring the marriage into holy matrimony. It is required that both partners take the marriage vows gravely, and have a deep respect and consideration for the feelings of your spouse.

It matters to Jesus how you feel and what you think. He loves His church so much. Not only did He lay down His life for His bride, the church, but also He is presently interceding on the behalf of His church.

My sisters you represent value, beauty and durability. I remember hearing Mahalia Jackson sing during my childhood, "How I got over; how I got over; my soul looks back and wonders how I got over." Another songwriter said, "While we are trying to figure it out, God has already worked it out."

Only God can take black sin, wash it, and make it whiter than snow by using His red blood as the cleansing agent. Not only does God collect and store His jewels but also He is the jeweler who cares for the jewels. He prepares and cares for them. When it is your season, the Lord will set you in place. Just wait on Him and let Him order your steps. He is the ready artisan that prepares His jewels. He does not allow anyone else to handle His jewels. He may grant permission for you to be buffeted in order to complete the polishing process.

"The sheep follow Him: for they know His voice. And a stranger will they not follow." (John 10:4b, 5a). He removes the flaws, cuts away the rough edges, smoothes, polishes his jewels, and puts them in the right setting to display their beauty. Although satan desires to sift you as wheat, he cannot touch you unless the Master gives permission. Consider Job's situation.

One day God is going to open up His jewelry box and your brilliance will shine forth. It will be your season, because you honor the Lord, you fear Him and call upon the name of Jesus. He has claimed you as His personal possession. You are valuable. He created you the way you are. There is not another jewel in the world with the exact same facets and flaws that you have. You are unique. You are peculiar, as in special, not odd. No two jewels are prepared in the exact same way.

If you do not take the test, you do not have a testimony. God is making and molding us after His will. When you are going thru the fire, (the bad times, the hard times, the painful and hurting times, the times of despair), remember that God is with you in the fire. "If it be so, our God whom we serve is able to deliver us from the burning fiery furnace, and he will deliver us out of thine hand, O king." (Daniel 3:17)

I must tell you that sometimes we stay in situations longer than God would like for us to because we are "slow learners", and disobedient children. We prolong the agony by not following the instructions given to us in the Word of God. Instead of listening to the leading of the Holy Ghost, we put Him on mute, and then we proceed to follow the way we want to go instead of the way God would have us to go. Those are the times that the Lord employs tough love and looks at us from a distance in order for us to find our way back to His will.

After He brings you out, let go of past events. They are just stepping-stones to the top. You may have heard the song about the old goat that fell into a well. The farmer tried all he knew to get him out of the well. After numerous attempts, he decided to bury him in the well, but every time he threw a shovel full of dirt on that old goat, he would shake it off and trample it under his feet, and that pile of dirt kept getting higher, until the old goat just stepped out of the well onto dry ground.

You do the same. Shake it off and trample it under your

feet. Let God fight your battles. He will take care of those who use you and abuse you. "The battle is not yours, but God's." (2 Chronicles 20:15b). Get your spirit right. Do what you are supposed to do. Seek after the Lord. Keep your eyes on the prize. Do not look at the problem. Focus on the problem-solver. Remember the God of your salvation. Remember, the battle is not yours. It is the Lords. Serve Him in the beauty of holiness. Vengeance belongs to God. Wait on the Lord. "They that wait upon the Lord shall renew their strength. They shall mount up with wings as eagles. They shall run, and not be weary. They shall walk and not faint." (Isaiah 40: 31).

The enemy loves to trap us and lead us into oppression, depression and digression, but look to the Lord. "The joy of the Lord is your strength." (Nehemiah 8:10b) Do not be timid and fearful. You must be courageous.

NOTES

_____

_____

_____

_____

_____

The Way Out

When you are trying to listen to several people at one time, it is easy to get confused. You have to be single-eyed, thereby being single-minded. Stay focused. Jesus said my sheep know my voice and that of another they will not hear. To whom are you listening? Are you listening to your tormenter? We know he is an accuser of the brethren. Do not listen to the one that is trying to condemn and discourage you.

You can never satisfy some people, no matter what you do. I cannot tell you how many times I was told I was of no use to anyone and I could not think off the end of my nose. I was constantly berated and belittled. Compliments were rare. I would keep the house extraordinarily clean, and have meals prepared even when my husband would not eat at home because I thought I could satisfy him, and keep reproach away from me. I was listening to the voice of my tormenter instead of my shepherd. I started believing a lie. Because a person describes you in a negative way does not necessarily mean you are who they say you are. Who does God say you are?

We must not look for the arms of flesh to give us answers to our problems. Our friends can sometimes be of solace to us but in the end, we must seek the Lord for guidance. No one else can tell you how to live your life or make things right for you. I was guilty of seeking sympathy from people by telling them my problems. For some reason, I thought someone would be able to tell me what to do, and help me align my life with the Word of God and make my marriage what I felt it should be. People do not have the answers. They have their own problems with which to contend.

Only God can help us through life's challenges. His Word is our guide. The Holy Spirit is our teacher. The Word and the Holy Spirit are activated and motivated through praying in faith. Prayer does not change God, it changes you, so you can receive what God has for you.

There was a song some years ago, entitled "Is God Satisfied with me?" My spouse would play it frequently. I do not know if he was playing it for himself or for me. I do know God is foremost. He is the one we are to seek to satisfy. God is first. Oswald Chambers says, "He is the utmost." He is our creator and reason for being. We were created for His glory. Do not listen to your oppressor. Listen to the voice of the good shepherd and you will know when to step out of the darkness. You will know when to step thru that door! Jesus is the door. He is THE WAY OUT.

Jesus sent the comforter to lead and guide us into all truth. What is the truth? Jesus is the truth. Is the truth, the fact that you were put on the earth to be tormented and confused? Is the truth, the fact that you are being or have been abused and molested? Is the truth, the fact that every time you think you are coming out, you allow something or someone to drag you back in? No, that is not the truth. "And you shall know the truth, and the truth shall make you free." (John 8:32)

In spite of your circumstances, you can still be free. You can acquire all of the fruit of the Spirit and walk in peace and victory. You can live your life without being consumed by the circumstances. When you are free, you are not bound or enslaved to what is being manifested around you. The craziness being manifested in your life does not have to have an adverse effect upon you.

You must know who you are in Christ. Learn to see yourself as God sees you. You were created for His glory, not some man's glory. Christ liberated women. He recognized them as individuals who could be included in His kingdom rather than chattel to be used, bought and sold. He included them rather than excluding them. You are to be honored and respected. You are equal to any other human being in the spiritual realm. God does not see you as more than or less than any other man or woman.

You are made in the image of God. Genesis 1:27 lets us know He made both male and female in His image. The fact that man was made first does not mean he is superior. I like to think that God saved the woman for last because He wanted all of creation to be in place when He bought her forth, so she would be provided for sufficiently as the weaker vessel. She did not have to want for anything. That relationship should be personified in the marriage relationship. The way that Christ loves the church, is the way the husband should love his wife. It is a sacrificial, giving love, and the wife is to be submissive to her husband. Submissiveness does not infer the harshness and severity that accompanies servitude as the world sees it, but a voluntary giving of yourself by putting your husband first and honoring him as the priest of your home, and the head of the household. Always have his well-being at heart. Care for him in every way.

Authority and power flow from servant hood. They do not automatically come from position. There is great responsibility and obligation involved. The authority of the husband means he should be reliable, dependable, and able to act on behalf of his wife, since it is God's plan that he is the head of his home. Some have grasped the part about being the head, without receiving the full revelation of honoring the wife and loving her as Christ loved the church, which is sacrificially.

If you are in Christ, you are no longer in bondage to sin, whether it is yours, or someone else's. On August 12, 2003, I was reviewing my life and realized I had run away from my home at least seven times (as far as I could remember.) I know seven is symbolic of God's number of completion. Holy Spirit was leading me to press toward the mark for the high calling and not to look back. It was time for me to grow up.

The devil wants to kill, steal and destroy. He wants to stop you from fulfilling God's plan for your life. Have you put your hopes and dreams on the shelf for someone else's selfish ambitions? Your life can be balanced and complete in Jesus. You can be a child of God, a wife, a mother and whatever else God has ordained for your life. He said, "Before I formed thee in the belly, I knew thee." (Jeremiah 1:5)

I must reiterate, because sometime it is so easy for others to come to an incorrect conclusion. I know a wife is to submit herself to her husband. There is a difference to submitting to your husband and submitting to those ungodly spirits that are driving him. The husband is to love his wife as Christ loved the church. Some men do not grasp the significance of that passage. The husband has a very weighty role. Christ gave His life for the church. He is in a perpetual courtship with the church. He is intercessor for the church. That means He is still our go between, our mediator. He is at the Father's right hand pleading our cause at all times. The church is of utmost importance to Him.

I am so glad to be a woman. God has placed a great charge upon the man. It is also a great responsibility that He has placed on the woman. The beautiful thing is He has given us all we need to achieve all He has destined for us. We must know who we are in Christ, before we can realize who we are in this earthly realm.

Did I miss something? Does the Word tell us to honor, obey and be submissive to our husband while it tells him to LOVE his wife? Think about that. We are to have love one to another, but when admonishing the husband on several occasions it strongly suggests he is to love his wife even to the degree that he loves her as he loves himself. The wife is to become one with her husband. Who in their right mind would harm himself? When a husband loves his wife the way God ordained it, he will encourage her to be all she can be in Christ. He becomes her savior. A savior rescues from harm or danger. He does not inflict harm or danger. When this principle is fully manifested within the marriage relationship, it is so very easy for the wife to succumb to the authority of her husband. There is no daily struggle and conflict. They can confront life together instead challenging each other.

A mature Christian wife knows she is to take care of home first and then she can be involved in other activities. Society has evolved to the extent that women often have to work outside the home in order to help provide a satisfactory quality of life. She should have some say in how the finances of the family are to be handled, even if she does not have a job. I will even venture to say that all the household duties should be shared to a certain extent if both spouses are working outside the home. Since she and her spouse are one, they should share in the planning and preparation for running the household. Ultimately, the husband is to see that his family is provided for and their needs are met. He is to discuss the affairs of the family with his wife, not treat her as though she is an indentured servant.

I once had dreams of becoming a concert pianist. I once had dreams of traveling the world. After over forty years of not studying or practicing, I cannot play one classical piece from memory, and I do not do well in sight-reading music either. I have acquired a degree in music education with piano as my major, but that dream was allowed to die. I allowed that dream to be killed, because I had lost my focus and allowed my priorities to be pushed aside. I did not seek God's will for my life. I did not know how. That may or may not have been His purpose for me. The point is, I was not in Christ, and I was not seeking the will of God.

Now in the autumn of my life, God has allowed other hopes and dreams to come alive in my spirit. He has appointed me to exhort and teach the Word of God and to be an encourager to hurting, bruised women. The things I experienced have become stepping-stones to a needed ministry. I want to share what God has birthed in me, so my sisters will find THE WAY OUT.

NOTES

_____

_____

_____

_____

_____

_____

_____

Running

#1 - I ran out into the dark rainy streets of Chicago one night. I was running away from a loud, threatening, menacing spouse. I went to a movie until he fell asleep in a drunken stupor. My babies had not been born yet. This was probably the early part of 1966.

#2 - I fled to a police station in Washington, D.C. I was fleeing from a drunken, raging companion. A police officer returned with me to our apartment but my husband denied us entry because we did not have a search warrant. I sat in the police station until my mother wired some money to me, and then I went to a motel until I felt it was safe to return home, after talking to my husband on the telephone. The night before, he had placed his police special under his pillow and told me if I had not given the right answers to his questions, he would have blown my head off. My babies were in bed in the next room. My son was five and my daughter was two and a half years old. This was probably around 1971.

#3 - I ran out of the house in Maryland, one rainy night. I was barefooted, and dressed in my nightgown and robe. Nothing but the grace of God kept me from cutting my bare feet when I hid behind a building three blocks away from my home. After about an hour, I returned to the house. He (my husband) was asleep. I believe that was somewhere in the mid-seventies. My children were upstairs in bed.

#4 - While still living in Maryland, I threw luggage out a second story window (my son's bedroom window), while my spouse was in the basement sleeping in front of the television after being away from home all weekend. This was a regular occurrence. I was supposed to be going to church, but I drove my children to St. Louis, Missouri. I believe my son was in Junior High School and my daughter was in the fifth grade, so that would have been approximately 1978. He finally contacted me after two or three weeks and came to where we were. He was baptized at the little church where I had grown up and we renewed our vows. Beware of the wiles of the devil.

This was the third marriage ceremony. The first was a civil ceremony in the Chicago, Illinois Cook County Court House. The second ceremony was in my mother's garden in Kirkwood, Missouri. It was truly esthetically captivating, but that does not make the marriage successful.

The fourth ceremony was somewhere around 1992 in Wilmington, North Carolina. The fifth ceremony was a remarriage in North Carolina, after he divorced me in 1997. He had the nerve to be offended when I would not have another wedding ceremony in 2000 when we were living in

Dolton, Illinois. What was the purpose? With all the evil and darkness that was perpetrated in our lives, the ceremonies were just a mockery of holy matrimony. A marriage ceremony will not make you and your spouse become one. You become one through the Holy Spirit, not man's spirit. By being obedient to God, you come into Holy Matrimony.

#5 - My husband's aunt was visiting us in Washington, D.C. We were riding around sightseeing before taking her to the train station. We were drinking alcoholic beverages. The conversation became quite intense and one word led to another. He told me to shut up and I would not, so he backhanded me in the mouth. I do not remember what the conversation was concerning.

It was supposed to be a conversation involving everyone, but he wanted me to be quiet so he could talk. I was really frightened. I jumped out of the car with his aunt when we arrived at the train station, under the pretense of walking her to the train. I boarded the train with her and went to Chicago. I was afraid to return to the car because I knew he was angry and out of control and I feared what might happen when there was no one around to witness his actions. I ended up in St. Louis again, where I allowed him to come and get me, after a few weeks. I believe this occurred in 1979. It seems as though these violent confrontations were occurring on what seemed a yearly basis.

#6 - I ran to a neighbor's house in distress and returned home later in the day when an Elder from the church we were attending called me, after my husband called him. The minister convinced me to return home, because I had received the Holy Ghost that month and he convinced me that I should not be afraid. My husband had placed his 38 revolver on the kitchen counter and wanted me to "come up with some money." This was in July of 1981. I had received the Holy Ghost on July 6, 1981, while he was on vacation and had spent all of his money. When he came to me for money, I had spent all I had and I guess he felt either I was lying or if he scared me enough I would "come up" (his words) with some money.

#7 - I went to work one day and did not return home at the end of the day after picking the children up from school. We stayed with a co-worker until we moved into an apartment in Columbia, Maryland. I had not been there a month when I allowed my husband to coerce me into returning home when I contacted him about getting some furniture from our house. This took place in the mid-eighties.

#8 - My husband was charged and convicted of molesting our daughter. During the period after being charged, and before he was sentenced, he busted in the basement door in order to gain entry into the house, so once again I fled. I moved to Annapolis, Maryland with my children (then ages 14 and 17). He was convicted. He was convicted and served time in Upper Marlboro, Maryland (public court records). The time-span was approximately 1984-1985. I allowed him to come back into the home when he was released and we moved to North Carolina in 1989. Both children were out of the home by this time.

#9 - In 1995 I left our home in Wilmington, North Carolina after threats and intimidation about finances again. I moved into an apartment for one year and then had a house built. It was during this separation that he divorced me. We remained apart until we remarried in 1998 and I left my house to go live with him in Illinois. Once more, someone from the church influenced me. You know the drill: "Shh! don't tell anybody what's going on in your home. We will pray about it. God will work it out. Your place is with your husband." Since then, I have learned that God can work anything out if you will allow Him to, but He will not defy your will.

#10 - By August of 2003, we were living in Pearl, Mississippi where we had purchased another house in 2001. Again, I left the home because of the many threats and arguments about finances. I tried seeking godly counsel, but it is necessary for both marriage partners to participate if it is going to be effective.

I will not have to run any more. I have found THE WAY OUT! - Not just in the natural, but spiritually as well. Leaving a physical location does not denote or signify deliverance. What is required is a total change or metamorphosis, if you will.

Through it all God kept me. As I continue to grow in grace and learn more of the Word, I become stronger and more enlightened. God's ways are not like man's ways. I now know that if I had received the Holy Ghost and walked in the power and anointing that was available to me and learned to pray, those many years of upheaval and turmoil in my life would not have prevailed for such a long length of time.

The Word does not become reality or act as a fulcrum or pivotal point in your life unless you immerse yourself in it and become fully engrossed or absorbed in it.

I realize that my weakness and lack of wisdom caused me to go through so much. My sisters please develop your relationship with the Lord before you try to develop a relationship with a man. Our flesh and the society around us tell us we need to develop a relationship with a man as soon as the hormones start kicking in. That is a lie from the pit of hell. The most prized and important thing in life is your soul's salvation. You do not have life (a life) if you do not have Jesus, the Christ.

Remember the Israelites and their march in the wilderness? It took them forty years to get to the Promised Land because they were not ready to enter in, spiritually. I believe because I did not walk in the Spirit, and I was carnal and self-centered instead of God-centered, God allowed me to continue in the wilderness. I did not release my marriage to Him. I tried to walk through it my way.

All of this confusion and calamity took place from 1962 when I met my husband while I was on vacation in Chicago with some of my college friends, until 2003, forty-one years later. I see the period from 1962 until 1965, when we had our first marriage ceremony as the courting, seducing years and from that time until the year 2003, as the time God was extending His grace and allowing me to find THE WAY OUT.

"Now thanks be unto God, which always causeth us to triumph in Christ, and maketh manifest the savour of his

26

knowledge by us in every place." (II Corinthians 2:14) God does not promise that we will not go through trials and tribulations, but He does promise He will go with us as we strive to overcome. We have the victory in Christ Jesus and because of this the knowledge that our relationship with Him imparts, gives us understanding of what could have been insurmountable. It is a supernatural occurrence. Natural laws are defied when we triumph in Christ.

NOTES

_____

_____

_____

_____

_____

_____

_____

_____

My Testimony

We are overcome by the blood of the lamb and the word of our testimony. I can testify to you with assurance that God is able to do exceeding, abundantly above all we could ever ask or think, according to the power that is working in us (See Ephesians 3:20). He can bring you out and He can bring you through, so that your marriage stays intact and becomes holy matrimony.

That was not the case for me. Some of us have gone through what we consider as hell on earth and have cried out many times: "Lord, don't you see what's going on? Where are you? Please deliver me."

I can remember sitting on my front porch until two or three o'clock in the morning, hoping my husband would come home, and he did not. I thought if I was awake and met him at the door; it would stave off the ferocious manner in which he would enter the house after he had been out drinking. After I finally went to bed, he would come in around five or six in the morning and holler at me to get up and fix him some food as he ranted and raged. Most of the time, he would fall asleep before I had finished preparing the food.

I was instructed to do what I was told if I was intending to stay in that house. When I would hear his key in the lock, my bowels would become loose because I did not know what I would have to confront when he came through the door. I do not intend to be crude or graphic but I am just illustrating to my sisters that is not the way to live your life. For any brothers that read this book I tell you that is not a marriage.

I can remember being told to shut up on numerous occasions and my opinion did not count. He would say if I wanted to express my opinion, tell it to someone else because he (my husband) was not interested. These are just a few of my memories. It is not essential for the purpose of this book, to relay everything. I have only given my perspective of what has happened in my life for the sake of helping others to find THE WAY OUT. Your perspective is your reality.

We traveled a lot, whether we had paid all of our bills or not. People only saw the traveling aspect as they received post cards from all across the United States. They could not see the fact that we were financially unprepared for vacation, and I was often an unwilling participant. I was not usually given the choice of where we were going, or even if I wanted to go. In my ignorant state of bliss, it never occurred to me that I should be involved in the decision-making. I was just so happy to be married to this good-looking man, have children and travel all across the

United States.

Most of the time the children and I were "dumped" at a relatives home while he went out and did his thing, whatever that was. We almost never stayed in a motel. Being young, uninformed and inexperienced, I was just glad to be going on a trip, per se. I was surprised to learn after about nineteen years when I started venturing out more when we traveled, that many people did not know whose wife I was because we very seldom did anything together. Some said they did not know my husband had a wife. I was generally restricted to whatever house we were staying in, while continuing to prepare meals and do the same things I would have done had I stayed at home. That was not a vacation to me.

Why am I remembering so much at this time? I would say that most of the information included in this book, I had forgotten until I started journaling. It needed to be remembered so I could be healed, and thereby bring healing to others. I have internalized so much that needs to be discarded. Until recently, I would try to put the past out of my mind, only to find that whenever it was brought up in conversation or I saw or heard something that jogged my memory, I would have nightmares, and my spirit would become very disturbed and troubled. For a long time, I was very fearful.

I still have flashbacks but they are no longer fearful to me. When they come, it is just an occasion to give thanks to God. I can lie down and rest in peace because I have found THE WAY OUT.

My sisters that have gone through and the ones that are still going through, you too can find THE WAY OUT. It is also my prayer that any male that has perpetrated his way into the church (building) and has seen himself in any part of this book, will repent and find THE WAY OUT.

I must clarify that finding THE WAY OUT does not mean finding your way out of your marriage if you are married. It represents finding your way out of darkness. THE WAY OUT may lead you out of a marriage but my prayer is that the marriage can be salvaged. No one wants his or her marriage vows to be dissolved and it is definitely not the will of God.

NOTES

_____

_____

_____

_____

_____

_____

_____

Hold on and look up my sisters, the time is at hand. When your time for deliverance comes, be ready to step through the door. You will shine as one of the most beautiful jewels God has. You will become dazzling and significant. Everything will take on a fresh, wholesome meaning. You will walk in the newness of life.

I am not trying to place the blame anywhere else or deny the fact that I allowed myself and my children to be consumed by what was happening in my life. I may never know why I jeopardized the well-being of my children repeatedly. I can truthfully say without exaggerating that my children and I have a very close, loving relationship now. If they are holding anything against me, it is not evident. I do not detect any bitterness or resentfulness on their behalf. We seem to have a mutual concern for each other's well-being. I know many are wondering if they have a relationship with their dad. The answer is no. I doubt if he even knows where they live, unless someone else has told him.

I do know that God is merciful and long-suffering. His grace and mercy has kept us. Man may look at me cross-eyed and I venture to say that some are baffled, but I truly believe this is the season for uncovering, at any cost. I will elaborate on that concept in another chapter.

The truth must be told. That is the only way deliverance will come. It is not about living in a beautiful, well-furnished home, taking a long vacation every year, getting a new car every few years, wearing nice clothes, or looking like the family from "Father Knows Best", which is deceptive. It is about my soul's salvation. I want to be ready when my time comes to depart from this world.

I strongly believe that no matter what we go through, certain situations in life are a testimony and help us to mature. We may bring trauma and drama into our lives, but God can use it to mature us.

Pride rears its ugly head in many different ways. Pride will keep you in bondage when you are more afraid of what people will say, than you are afraid of not being obedient to what God has ordained for your life. There are times now when the enemy tries to make me feel guilty and ashamed. People have asked me numerous times, usually in a condescending way, "Why did you keep going back to him? What was the matter with you?" Proverbs 11:2 tells us "When pride cometh, then cometh shame: but with the lowly is wisdom". "He that soweth to his flesh shall of the flesh reap corruption." (Galatians 6:8) When you sow carnality, you reap carnality.

To this present day, I have to stay prayerful because shame and guilt will try to creep in. Fear rears its ugly head from time to time. While I am writing this book, the enemy is trying to make me overly concerned about what my husband's reaction will be. My first priority is throwing out a lifeline to my sisters that are still in bondage. I want to do the will of God.

"There is therefore now no condemnation to them which are in Christ Jesus, who walk not after the flesh, but after the Spirit. For the law of the Spirit of life in Christ Jesus hath made me free from the law of sin and death." (Romans 8:1-2) I am minding the things of the Spirit. I have a debt to pay. I have not received the spirit of bondage again to fear.

It is so easy to quote scriptures, but they must become rooted and grounded in our Spirit and implanted in our heart. Let them take seed and germinate. Our response to the Word must be so embedded that their significance and meaning stimulates a reflex that is automatic, when we encounter each day's adversities.

I believe I was looking for a father figure. I did not grow up with my father. The only male in the house was my grandfather, who was very sick with asthma. Although he was physically incapacitated, he dispensed love by giving what he could to the household financially. I can truthfully say I did not want for anything as a child. I do not remember having any conversations with him about life. He would often send me to the store for him or say something in his very colorful way, when he saw someone in the household acting unseemly. I do not remember him giving any sage advice. He spent most of his time in his bedroom or sitting in a corner of the dining room, near a heating vent, trying to stay warm. He passed away during my first year in college. I really did not know what was expected of the male head of the household. When my grandmother, who passed away when I was twelve years old, was living, she acted as head of the household. After her demise, my mother became head of the household.

I believed all the chauvinistic rhetoric of the world. We were a house full of women. Our household consisted of my grandparents, one of my aunts and her daughter, another cousin that my grandparents raised and my mother and I. The aunt that was living there married while I was still a young girl, and my other cousin married and moved out as well. That left my mother and I after both of my grandparents were deceased.

My mother and I were very close. She was my mother and my friend. She nurtured me and loved me in every way she knew how. She was very protective; therefore, I was not exposed to the hardships and inconsistencies of life. She saw that I had everything I needed and wanted. I was told she divorced my father when I was a baby. He provided child-support until I was eighteen but I never knew him personally. She had three other marriages but I never had a father-daughter relationship with any of her husbands and she was indeed the matriarch of the home.

My mother worked more than one job to be sure my needs were met. I always had an abundance of things. After graduating from high school, I was given an ultimatum of going to college or moving out of the home immediately. Of course, I chose college. I wanted a job while in college but her statement was "I sent you to college to learn. Your job is to bring home A's and B's."

It is imperative that you make Jesus the center of your life. You cannot wander through life aimlessly expecting people or things to fulfill or complete that vacant spot that was created only for God to occupy. Material things will not do it. Temporal things will not satisfy or fill the longing that is deep within your soul. Relationships with those around you will only come into alignment if your connection to God is in order.

Another reason I think I was so vulnerable is I was a virgin when I met my husband, and because of my being so na-ïve, I was susceptible to his wiles and innuendos. He is the only man I have ever known sexually. The sex drive is very strong and compulsive. When young people start developing in this area, they are often overwhelmed with the flood of emotions and sensations they have never experienced before. It is essential that parents educate their children and prepare them so they will not be ensnared. Many lives have been adversely altered by not being aware of the consequences of what is inappropriate behavior.

You must know who you are before you can attempt to know someone else. Most young women of my generation wanted to grow up, get married, and have two children, two cars and a house. One thing is certain, you must examine yourself and know what your motives are for wanting to enter into a relationship with a man. Your motives must be pure. Is your reason for establishing a relationship to be a part of the in-crowd? Do you want to get married because your friends are marrying? Are you curious about sex? Do you just want to get away from home and have someone else take care of you, or do you want to live up to the image that society has projected?

I may never fully know the answer, but I do know that I thank God I am not where I should be, but I am not where I used to be.

There must come a time when you will step out and stand flat-footed and firm against the wiles of the devil. How do you do that? Where does the strength come from? "I can do all things through Christ which strengtheneth me." (Philippians 4:13). If you yield to the attacks of the devil, you will continue to plummet into a state of darkness and despair. It is like a never-ending roller coaster.

At this point, I must reiterate that the purpose of this book is to bring deliverance and encouragement to my sisters. No one should have to live in a daily atmosphere of contempt and hopelessness. I never shared this with anyone before, because I believe I was living in denial, but there were times I considered going to the Bay Bridge and driving into the Chesapeake Bay. Now that I have found THE WAY OUT, I know that Jesus came to give us life and that more abundantly. I know it deep down in my soul, and not just intellectually, that we can awaken each day to a new hope and joy as we look forward to what the Lord has in store for us.

How do you prepare your defenses? You do that by fasting, praying, and staying in the Word. Let us look at Ephesians 6:10-18. We are told to gird up and put the armor of God on. Did you notice that a passage of scripture about wives and husbands, children and parents, slaves and masters comes before the passage about wearing the whole armor of God? It is all about submissiveness in your personal relationships. The revelation I received from this is, wrong relationships can wound, hurt, maim, distort, disfigure and even kill. The armor is to protect you. The song says, "Can't nobody do you like Jesus". When your vertical relationship with God is right, you will consequently, get your horizontal relationships in order.

We finite humans cannot understand all of the authoritative commands of God. The reality of it is we are not supposed to. It is important that we obey the Word of God. We have learned from the story of King Saul in 1 Samuel 15:22, to obey is better than sacrifice. We are saved by grace, not works. No matter what we think we are sacrificing, we must do it God's way. Jesus paid the biggest sacrifice of all. We owe Him everything, yet we can never repay Him. The beauty of it is He does not expect us to do anything but love Him. Everything we do should evolve from that love.

I must say I have found a hiding place in Christ Jesus. No one can any longer convince me that I am not good for anything or of no use to anyone.

I am one of God's jewels. He has put me into his jewelry box for safekeeping. No hurt or pain can overcome me. I am in a safe place.

Once you have prayed and sought the Lord, you must then act according to the leading of the Holy Spirit. As a new creature in Christ, you must forsake the old ways, "And have no fellowship with the unfruitful works of darkness, but rather reprove them, For it is a shame even to speak of those things which are done of them in secret." (Ephesians 5:11-12) "See then that you walk circumspectly, not as fools, but as wise, redeeming the time, because the days are evil." (Ephesians 5:15-16)

When flashbacks come, triggered by something you see or hear, just fortify yourself by being instant in prayer. Philippians 4:6-8 tells us how to fortify our minds. Do not be sidetracked. Prayer is the glue that holds the armor together. We must think on good things. Do not dwell on negative, bad things. Do not entertain the devil. Give no place to the devil. The Word is our sword. It is our mode of defense. That is why it is referred to as a sword. In order to use a sword defensively you have to pick it up. An intruder will not be frightened or intimidated because you have a sword lying on the table.

I remember attending a women's service in North Carolina and the speaker said that many times we allow the devil to perch on our shoulder and whisper into our ear and instead of pushing him off, we get so engrossed in what he is saying that we put lipstick on him. It sounds humorous but it is realistic.

I allowed the enemy to tell me I had not forgiven, but I realized I was being fed a lie when I read the court papers from Wilmington, North Carolina for 1997. I was reading them in the year 2003 because my husband said he was divorcing me again and I was putting works with my faith by accumulating any information available that would be required of me in court, as the Holy Spirit was leading me. Do not be ignorant of the devils devices .We must watch and pray! The devil does not play fair.

There was so much that I had forgotten as I strived to make our marriage work. That is how I recognized the lie I was being fed about not forgiving. I had put it all out of my memory bank. I was not holding any animosity in my heart. When we forgive, we do not hold the person accountable. We start with a clean slate. Each time I would go back, hoping for a new start and satan would eventually rear his ugly head again.

The same tactics that had been used against me in 1995-1997, were being ushered forth in 2003:

1. The withholding of all my personal property, including

not having any thing in my name

2. The threats, harassment and intimidation leading to separation

3. The withholding of money; both mine and his, with him controlling all funds. (I kept the checkbook records but I was not at liberty to use it as I willed, because no allotment was made in the budget for tithes, offerings, food, clothing, gas, and miscellaneous items.)

4. Previously, he tried to turn our daughter against me by feeding her false information. This time he tried to seduce our son through frequent phone calls, which was indeed a new tactic, because he never called him in the past. When that tactic did not work, and he could not gather any information about me, he ceased calling him completely and has not answered or returned any calls our son makes to him. I believe that because of past events, he definitely will not call our daughter.

5. The attempt to receive a portion of my retirement funds

None of these things worked. I know that Holy Ghost will lead you and guide you into all truth. The Lord orders the steps of a good man (woman). (See Psalms 37:23) No weapon that is formed against me shall prosper; and every tongue that rises against me in judgment shall be condemned. (See Isaiah 54:17) The Lord will fight my battles.

Many other occurrences resurfaced in my mind while writing this book. Including them would not promote the purpose of this book, which is to heal, deliver, and to let my sisters know there is A WAY OUT. You are not alone. You are not the only one going through. Some of you have gone through trying, harrowing circumstances. I am not promoting separation or divorce. I am promoting making God the head of your family, walking in victory and praying through.

When the volcano was about to erupt in 2003, I suggested to my husband that we meet with our Pastor for counseling. As usual, he wanted no part of it. I had tried to get him into counseling in years past, to no avail. I do not know why he would not go. In 2003, he told me to go, but do not mention his name. He consented to meet with the Pastor and me when Pastor contacted him and asked him specifically to come in. At this particular meeting, the Lord pulled the covers off the fact that he was planning to leave me on August 10, 2003. God just totally uncovered his game plan.

I must stress, "Jesus Christ is the same yesterday, and today, and forever." (Hebrews 13:8) He never changes. His principles are yes and amen but since we are earthen vessels with the capability of constantly vacillating from one condition to another both in the natural and in the spiritual realm, we sometimes flow from one phase of our life to another without considering the severity of what we are doing. We must learn to be "steadfast, unmoveable, always abounding in the work of the Lord."(See 1 Corinthians 15:58) Do not let circumstances dictate to you or control you.

There was a period from 2003 until 2006 when I could not work on this book. I had to lay it aside and wait for the prompting of the Holy Ghost. I know it was because God was healing me. I had to allow him to remove all the bad spirits from me. I could not do a work for the Lord while I was angry, bitter, hurt and confused. The works of the enemy no longer frustrate me. The year 2003 is past, but the healing process had to become whole within me before I could complete this book.

I often pray for my husband. I know it is God's will that every man (woman) be saved. I pray he will repent and get in right relationship with the Lord. When he repents, I will know it, because he will reach out and ask for forgiveness from those whose lives he has affected in a bad way.

Now, when I consider the events that have taken place in my life, I can continue to pray for my husband. I no longer feel all of the adverse feelings I used to feel when I heard about him or thought about him. I wish no harm on him.

Let us review Ephesians the sixth chapter. After Paul writes about how the relationships mentioned in previous verses are supposed to be, he says in Ephesians 6:10, "Finally"! He knew that not all relationships are according to God's plan. Unfaithfulness, mistrust, doubt, perversion, incest, fornication, adultery, abuse, misuse, lying, cheating, threats, intimidation, aggressiveness, violence, controlling, manipulating and many other works of the flesh come into play. Oh yes, do not think because no physical force was used, that abuse did not take place. The tongue can maim, scar and kill. Being denied love will make your soul shrivel up and die or wish you were dead.

Being constantly criticized and ignored can make you curl

up into a ball and distance yourself from those around you. A constant barrage of threats and intimidation can really boggle your mind. In an effort to protect yourself you learn to "tune-out" what is going on around you. It is a way of not having to face reality when it becomes overwhelming. A tumultuous relationship with your spouse will confuse your mind to the extent that you cannot think straight or make wise decisions. When you are concerned about day-to-day survival, and getting from point "A" to point "B" you tend to be an animated robot, functioning by remote control.

You become an emotional and mental invalid. I became so good at "tuning-out" my spouse that I did not hear what he said half of the time. I could not retain it because it usually was something that caused me pain and distress emotionally and mentally. He often accused me of not re-membering things and he was right, because I had learned not to listen to him too closely because I could not tolerate many things he would say, and I did not understand most of what he said. If he kept talking persistently and aggres-sively, as he often did, it only served to confuse me and make my thinking more foggy and unclear.

Presently, I am trying to over-come that bad habit because I find myself not being a good listener to others. I had allowed myself to become so self-absorbed that I could not focus on the needs of others. My spirit had become calloused. I had to pray for God to take away the heart of stone and give me a heart of flesh.

I encountered all of this turmoil during the past forty years. There are those that try to characterize abuse as being a physical manifestation only. Abuse can also be emotional and mental. Any time you use a person or thing for a purpose other than what it was created for, it can become abuse.

There is no pain like the pain of being told your husband has been charged with molestation, and it becomes doubly painful when it is his own daughter. There is no pain like your son taking his father to court for physical abuse. Consider the effect of being kept awake all night while you are trying to console an inebriated, angry, aggressive husband and then you awaken your children for school and go off to teach other children, only to be told by your children when they become adults, that they were not asleep; they were in their beds cringing in fear and trying to sing themselves to sleep. Nothing but the grace of God can bring you through these types of situations.

I thank God that my children and I are closer together than ever and we usually talk several times a week. I cannot say their lives have not been affected in a negative way by what they experienced during their childhood. I trust the Lord to heal them day by day. I no longer try to act as a mediator between them and their dad. I no longer have to try to keep the peace in the house. I have turned all of our lives over to God. I know He is able to heal and restore. My son and daughter are grown and living their own lives now. It is my prayer that they will seek the Lord Jesus Christ. He can make all things right. No matter what occurs in life, he can give you "the peace of God which passeth all understanding." (See Philippians 4:7)

I still ponder over the question that has been asked of me many times, as to why I kept going back. I believe it was because of the pride of life. I wanted so much for my family to be ideal. I wanted to look good in the communities' eyes, not realizing that others saw what I could not see. I deceived myself into believing a lie. I was weak. I did not have enough Word in me to take a stand and hold firm.

I catered to my flesh. I had not allowed the Word to be sown in my heart (see Matthew 13). I thought I could look good to others, so I perpetrated a lie in my daily life. I became good at pretending.

I was that proverbial ostrich with my head stuck in the sand. I just did not believe there was that much evilness existing in my home. I wanted so much for my marriage to succeed.

I do not like these new so-called reality shows. To me, they are just legalized trash, but life has taught me we must face reality in our daily lives. We must not deceive ourselves into thinking the things that are taking place in our life are all right when they really are not. This "dumb" flesh will rationalize anything in order to feel comfortable and secure. It will tell you that things are not as bad as they seem. This type of thinking is not what the scripture means when it says "and calleth those things that be not, as though they were." (Romans 4:17) Do not misapply the Word in order to try to validate your circumstances.

"Study to show thyself approved unto God, a workman that needeth not to be ashamed, rightly dividing the Word of truth." (1Timothy 2: 15). If you know the Word for yourself, you will know right from wrong. You will know the will of God and you will know who you are in Christ, thereby distinguishing the "Good News" (the Gospel) from man's laws or philosophies.

This is not an indictment against the church. It is an admission of error and weakness on my part, by not allowing the Word to strengthen me in my inner parts so I could stand against the wiles of the devil and quench his fiery darts. Do not look to others for deliverance. God will make you free when you look to Jesus. He came to set the captives free.

No matter how much your family and friends love you, they cannot remove the vicissitudes of life from the path you choose to walk on.

When you do not know who you are in Christ, you not only deny yourself the benefits that come with salvation, but those in your intimate circle suffer as well. Your children, your immediate family and others receive the consequences of destruction and devastation of sin in the camp. There are sins of omission as well as sins of commission.

Sisters do not think that God does not see and hear. The church organization may turn its head. They may tell you to be quiet and not talk about it. They may encourage you to dress up, make-up and cover up just by their silence and unresponsiveness but you know that underneath is hurt, shame, guilt, bruises and festering sores. If something is not done about it, full blown cancer will develop. Nothing or no one can separate us from the love of God, which is in Christ Jesus our Lord.

NOTES

The Season For Uncovering

"This is the season for uncovering". I truly believe this is a word from the Lord. During this most recent conflict in 2003, "This is the season for uncovering", was a recurring theme, to the extent that I heard it in sermons and conversations of others. Many times as I listened to a radio or television broadcast, I would hear that phrase spoken.

Is there abuse and incest in the church? Yes there is! Talk to any Pastor that has been in the pulpit awhile. For some reason most churches have refused to recognize these maladies exist. The people whose lives have been touched by incest and abuse need ministering to. They cannot continue to be overlooked or ignored. It makes me think about "whited sepulchres."(See Matthew 23:24-28) My husband had an aunt that used to say, "Tell the truth and shame the devil". Alternatively, it seems the church is saying, "Tell the truth and shame the victim".

I understand that you have to use wisdom when addressing certain issues in the church, because everyone in the congregation does not possess the same amount of spiritual maturity, therefore you have to proceed with caution and be very prayerful, so the immature ones will not suffer any adverse effects.

Many people have been injured and therefore, ran away from the church because a brother or sister lacked wisdom in relating to them, so I definitely understand a Pastor's concern in approaching certain problems, but the Bible does give us a guide. 1 Corinthians chapters 5 and 6 are a good place to start.

Why are we willing to teach and preach about fornication, adultery, gambling, pornography on the internet, materialism and other sins? I have yet to hear a sermon addressing incest or molestation, and I have been in church a long time. What are we afraid of? It seems to be easier to address giving or the lack there of. I have heard numerous sermons on that topic, along with not spending enough time praying or reading the Word, which indeed are essential to spiritual growth. Some of the same ills that are prevalent in society also exist in the church. We must address those sins as well.

We must not allow the devil to become safeguarded in God's Sanctuary. I know God will judge and separate the wheat from the tare, but until Jesus returns, He left His Word to lead and guide us into all truth. The Holy Spirit is our teacher. The Word and the Holy Spirit are one in the Godhead.

Look at the statistics on divorce in the church, as compared to the world. Consider how many lay members are leaving the church pews and going back to the bar stools. Have you seen the statistics on how many "men and women of the cloth," our clergy, are exiting the pulpit and entering the wrong bedroom? Our attitude seems to be, Shh! do not talk about it. Perhaps if we ignore it, it will go away or at least diminish. Pornography and sexual lust is in epidemic proportions. Be aware of what is going on around you. We are not supposed to be of the world but we are still in the world. "be ye therefore sober, and watch unto prayer." (1 Peter 4:7b)

The "priesthood" in the Roman Catholic Church has been in the media a lot in recent years. Some of the more prominent or well-known preachers of the evangelical churches have also made the news.

I believe there wouldn't be so many of these sexual sins being perpetrated in the religious community if the people in the churches were not so reluctant to acknowledge what is happening ,and develop an action plan to deal with it before the worldly media gets involved.

Some individuals seem to think they can hide on the internet or in areas and neighborhoods where they do not think their congregants will see them, but the eyes of the Lord are everywhere. Illegitimate births and homosexuality are skyrocketing in our churches. The world is not teaching about abstinence. It is teaching people to use a condom as an alternative. Our children are bombarded with this in the public schools as well as the media. This abhorrent teaching starts at a very early age in the schools, on television, in the newspapers, magazines, and on billboards.

The body of Christ needs to wake up and learn how to fight this battle. We cannot deliver and protect our children by ignoring the problem or trying to conceal it. Some have navigated around this dilemma by enrolling their children in private schools, but many in the church cannot afford academies or parochial schools.

Either we believe the Word or we do not. There is no gray area. We cannot straddle the fence. The book of Revelation tells us what God will do with those who are lukewarm (See Revelation 3:15-16).

I want to take a hallelujah break and say that Pastor's wives, preacher's wives, minister's wives, and those in leadership, who are the most visible, are the most vulnerable to the kind of torment and turmoil I have experienced. Why is this? It is because the congregation puts them outside the circle. They are either put on a pedestal out of reach or put under the pews out of sight. This group of elect women is proverbially not supposed to go through the same thing as other women. They are put in the position of suffering in silence because if they reveal what is going on, they are ostracized and made to bear the guilt of not being worthy of what the congregants deem as leadership. Respect is denied them. They must exemplify perfection and purity in every way.

Their home is to be holiness personified. If the wife is having problems then the consensus is their husband must not be worthy of his position, or that wife is some how in the wrong.

Our church leaders are God's foot soldiers. They are His servants. They are not God. They have to fight the same battles as everyone else. We must constantly pray for them. I am going to leave that alone because that is a book within itself.

If the church would learn to handle these situations in a biblical way and minister to those in need within the body of Christ, the world's media wouldn't have such a wealth of information to propagate and to cast disparaging comments all over television, radio and in the written media.

We would not have to go before the unjust judge if we followed scriptural guidelines. I tried to disclose to the church what was going on in my home, at an official board meeting once and I was told by that Pastor that I should not have publicly revealed what was happening in my home, even though I had met with he and his wife prior to the church meeting, to no avail. That Pastor just wanted to sweep the dirt under the rug and hope by walking on it, the pile would get smaller. At least that is the impression I received.

I have also experienced the fact that some men and women are in the pulpit for filthy lucre. If a person is putting a lot of money into the basket, taking that minister out to eat frequently and giving lavish gifts, that clergy is inclined to overlook peculiarities and subtle signs that something is off kilter. I have also observed that not everyone in the pulpit is qualified to counsel. They are only there to preach.

It is my desire that the Lord will use me to minister to others who have needs similar to those addressed in this book.

I want my Christian sisters and brothers to be a strong, vibrant force in the world. If we are spiritually weak and sick, that will not happen. We must build up our spiritual muscles.

Find someone you can talk to and confide in. You need someone to pray with you, and for you, instead of judge you, and criticize you. We need stronger, mature saints that can lift up and encourage one another instead of gossiping, often facetiously called sharing. Do no tear one another down. When you disparage a brother or sister in Christ, you are disparaging yourself, because you are all of one body. A three-fold cord is not easily broken. Let that three-fold cord be you, the person in need and the Holy Ghost.

I suggest that the person you confide in is not someone in your congregation because it has been my experience that most people are not able to share your burden without becoming opinionated. Let us be for real about this thing. Most people are not that strong. They have a tendency to take the information that you disclose to them and project themselves into that situation and then to start judging you accordingly. They may not intentionally judge or criticize you, but subconsciously they try to think what they would do if they were in the same situation. Many times, they will not be able to look you in the eyes after you have revealed your most intimate thoughts to them. Sometimes it is because they merely do not know how to respond. Neither will you be able to look them in the eyes because you will start wondering what they think about you. You will also start wondering who they shared your "business" with, because your best friend has a best friend who has a best friend, and so on. That is why it is so important to be able to take your burdens to the Lord and leave them there. You are the apple of his eye. He will not turn away or avert his eyes from you.

One of the tricks of the enemy is to divide and conquer. I have often been told to be quiet and "don't tell your business". I truly believe that if I had confided to a mature saint of God years ago, the period of tribulation and trials for my family wouldn't have been as intense and would not have lasted as long because the prayers of the righteous avails much. (See James 5:16) In addition, there is strength in unity.

God's kingdom here on earth, the church, is a body of believers. We are the called out ones. Each part of that body is designed to work with the other parts. If your toe sets up gangrene, your whole body can become infected.

Now it is time for us to stop preaching and teaching a good shouting message about what we can gain, and start relating to the pain that is sitting in our congregations. There are so many that need assurance and support from the body of Christ in order to complete the healing process. There are many whose lives are in turmoil and they do not know what to do or who to talk with. As long as we are divided and suspicious of each other, we will always be apprehensive and we will not edify and console one another. Slew-foot is on his job. Are we on ours?

I have seen young women that do not want to be a part of the organized church because the sisters they meet "put their tongue on them" instead of praying for them. In the May/June 2003 issue of The Pentecostal Assemblies of the World magazine, "Christian Outlook", the presiding prelate, Bishop Norman L. Wagner said, "Be relevant! Develop a worshipping church of Jesus our Lord. Be sensitive to the needs, hurts and hopes of our people, and then preach it." I fully comprehend that this can apply to the layman as well as the clergy.

Are we fulfilling our mission for healing and setting the captives free? Otherwise, are we sending them to the world's psychiatrist and family counselors? When the demoniac is exposed, do we usher forth deliverance or do we send him back into the caves of darkness where others will not see him? Do we try to conceal him from public view? Do we feel we have to look holy and we have to play the role that is stereotypically applied to the saints of God? Do we really know what our role or part is? Are we functioning the way we are supposed to?

Do we break the chains of bondage or do we have other priorities? Is an abundance of time spent holding an auction; excuse me, I meant collecting offerings? Do we spend more time collecting offering than we do laying hands and casting out demons? Some churches do not practice this ideology any more.

I know it takes money to help advance the Kingdom of God, but if the Word about tithing and offerings is taught in our bible studies and thereby reinforced within the body, then all we have to do is pass the basket. We will not have to hold $100, $50 or $10 lines. Giving should be a doctrinal teaching along with the baptism in Jesus' name and the baptism of the Holy Ghost.

The time is past due for "pumping up" the saints for worship and giving. Give them the Word and they will give to the Lord. I refuse to stand in one of those money lines referred to as offering lines, because I have purposed in my heart that I will always be a good steward of God's money. It is not mine. I am going to give as the Lord directs me regardless of who is collecting the offering and what is being said.

Praise and worship should not be a choreographed production led by a director or Holy Ghost drum major. During the devotional portion of the service, we should be preparing our spirits to receive the Word of God as we are offering up praises and worship to our God. There will be times when it is long. There will be times when it is short. It should be led by the unction of the Holy Ghost. Sometimes we are overly concerned about staying with the program. In spite of this, many times it seems that the Word is the shortest portion of our "order of service". We will need that sword when we confront the enemy when we leave the church service.

Let us spend less time doing our own typical or traditional thing. Let the Holy Spirit have free course in the services, and the people that need something besides emotionalism, and politics, will receive what they need, from the Lord. Before you go there, yes, I know God is about order, but it is His order, not ours.

We cannot continue to listen to feel good messages and pretend to shout it out and go back home in the same condition we came in. It is time for the body of Christ to minister to the whole person. While we are waiting for our deliverance, we must look to Jesus. He said He would never leave you nor forsake you. He said He would send the comforter. Boy, do a lot of us need comforting! Am I touching you in sensitive areas? I hope so. The Comforter will lead and guide us into all truth. Scripture says, "He sent His Word and healed them." This book will be an agent of healing also, because it is based upon the principles of God.

Someone once said, "Look around and be distressed. Look within and be depressed. Look to Jesus and be at rest."

Let us return to Ephesians 6:10-18. Sisters while you are waiting on the church to come to your assistance do everything you can to be in the will of God. What is the will of God for you? III John 2 says "Beloved, I wish above all things, that thou mayest prosper and be in health, even as thy soul prospereth." The qualifying phrase there is "even as thy soul prospereth." How does your soul prosper? Your soul prospers through the Word. Eat the Word. It is sweeter than a honey cone. Make your spirit fat. It will not allow bitterness, hurt, and shame to take root.

Eat the word. Hear the Word and speak the Word. However, best of all, be a doer of the Word. Let your life-style reflect the glory of the Word. A songwriter once said, "Get wrapped up, tied up and tangled up in Jesus." Do not worry about those that say it does not take all that. Work out your own soul's salvation with fear and with trembling. Save yourself from this untoward generation and pray, pray, pray! "Men ought always to pray, and not to faint." (Luke 18:1b) It takes all of that and then some more. Become unreservedly enthusiastic and passionate about your faith.

Daily communication with God is essential to our quality of life as a Christian.

Ephesians the sixth chapter tells us above all to take the shield of faith while praying and watching for all saints. These are the pivotal words in that passage. We must have complete trust in God and what Jesus did on the cross, which will lead us to the place where we will become our brothers or sisters keeper. (See Genesis 4:8-12)

For All I Trust Him (FAITH)! Believe that the Lord is a deliverer, a shield, a buckler and a present help in time of trouble. We must pray, pray, pray! Will talking on the telephone to a friend for hours help you or resolve the obstacles in your life? I seriously doubt it. That friend has problems and concerns also.

Pray without ceasing. Hoping is not praying. Turn your plate down. Turn the television off. Turn the ringer off on the telephone. Talk to God.

Pray for your sister that usually sits across the aisle from you, instead of whispering about her. You may call it sharing. No girlfriend, it is really gossiping. What you perceive as being anti-social may really be a protective shield to keep her from being hurt more than she is already hurting.

God's Word is more secure and firm than any church pew can ever be. I cannot say it enough, that you should not be a hearer of the Word only. You also must be a doer of the Word. Let it penetrate your soul and pervade throughout your entire being. Let the Word enlighten your mental faculties as well as your spirit. The Word of God must become the essence of who you really are. If you allow it to permeate your heart, when you hear it, it will cause an automatic reflex to take place when things are not as they should be, because the Holy Spirit will unction it.

Do not think God does not see what is going on behind closed doors. When we are in a difficult situation, we tend to forget that He is omnipotent, omnipresent and omniscient. The eyes of the Lord are everywhere. For those who are still carrying wounds and pain from childhood, stay focused. Remember the Word is a cleanser. It washes whiter than any fuller's soap. Give your hurt, your guilt, your pain and your insecurities to Jesus. Leave them at the altar. If you take them back home with you, they will fester and become foul smelling and full of putrefying pus. "But unto you that fear my name shall the Sun of righteousness arise with healing in his wings; and ye shall go forth, and grow up as calves of the stall." (Malachi 4:2)

NOTES

_____

_____

_____

_____

_____

_____

You must not take the responsibility for someone else and his or her actions. They may appear to be remorseful while the situation is close at hand, but then as time passes, they forget the gravity of their sin because you have not allowed them to take the brunt or consequences of their sin. As the embers of the fire cool, they become comfortable with where they are. Many times when they see the spirit of forgiveness in you, they take it for granted that all is well. If they do not have a repented heart, they see it as weakness. Now I realize why Paul said in 1 Corinthians 5:5 "To deliver such an one unto satan for the destruction of the flesh, that the spirit may be saved in the day of the Lord Jesus."

As you allow your burdens to accumulate, they will become overbearing. They will bury you. Take your burdens to the Lord and leave them there. Do not try worldly remedies for fighting the enemy, "for the children of this world are in their generation wiser than the children of light." (Luke 16:8b)

Some of us have become so good at covering up, that we are not even honest when we come to God in prayer. We try to look holy to the church and we do not seem to realize we cannot look holy to God. We can fool some of the people some of the time, but we can never fool God any time. The Word is "a discerner of the thoughts and intents of the heart." (Hebrews 4:12b)

The world says you need counseling, and you are scarred for life. God says you are a new creature in Christ. You are being made into the image of Christ. You do not belong to mother, daddy, husband, boss-man, your children or yourself. You were bought with a price. You were paid for with the precious blood of Jesus. You are God's creation. You are His precious possession. Learn to spend time with Him. Stay in His presence. Be malleable, and be where you are supposed to be, subsequently being in peace, you will find your place.

You are not responsible for the fact that mama was married four times or was not married at all, so you vowed that would never happen to you. You are not responsible because someone used you for his or her sex toy. Do not try to bear the burden of dysfunctional relationships, which are sinful relationships. You are a new creature in Christ.

If daddy was not there for you, God is. Jesus said, "Lo, I am with you always, even unto the end of the world." (Matthew 28:20). I grew up in a home without my dad. I was not allowed to have a relationship with him for whatever reason. He never reached out to me. He provided child support for me until I reached the age of consent, which during that time, was the age of eighteen. When I became an adult and had my own children, I tried to form a relationship with him. At first, he seemed willing to reciprocate, but I learned later that he told his wife that he doubted if I was his child and he would not come to the telephone whenever I called them. That devastated me.

I spent my early childhood in a home with my divorced mother, her parents and an unwed aunt who had one child at that time and another cousin whose mother had died. What effect did this have on me? I do not know. I believe I had a very good childhood. There was plenty of love in the home. I was taught to go to church and live an honorable life, but I did not know about committing my life to Jesus and living holy. In fact, my friends and I mocked those that were in holiness because they were different from us. I knew that all of my friends and those close to me went to church but I did not understand why it was so important. At that point, in my life, the church was a gathering place, a social club of sorts. I was not convicted in my heart; therefore, I was not converted.

I now realize that it was more or less an acceptable social activity. When I accepted Christ as my Savior, rather than seeing Him as a fictional character, I received a new family within the body of Christ, and my life took on new meaning. It was at that time that I realized that going to church was more than being morally good. It was about establishing a relationship with God through His only begotten son.

Because I am an only child, my immediate family is very small. The few cousins I am in contact with do not really see or talk to each other very often. I am not deprived of love by any stretch of the imagination. We reach out to each other occasionally but most of us never bonded together or established a close relationship. However, the Lord has blessed me with special, caring people in my life and my spiritual family is very extensive. I am in frequent contact with my sisters in Christ. We do not necessarily talk personal things, but we do encourage each other in the Word and in prayer as we lift up the name of Jesus.

If you are baptized with the Holy Ghost, He will lead you in your conversation, without you knowing that you are addressing a specific need at that time. I remember hearing some of the saints say: "Let go and let God." I believe I now understand what they were implying. When we relinquish our hold on something we think we have control of, release it, and God is able to work, but He will not defy your will.

Do not let the past weigh you down. While you are trying to figure it out, God has already worked it out. God allows you to go through certain situations so He may be glorified. I know there was nothing good about it, and the devil meant it for bad, but God can turn it into good. I know you remember Joseph. You have a testimony. Tell somebody about the goodness of the Lord. Tell how God delivered you.

"The kingdom of heaven suffereth violence and the violent take it by force."(Matthew 11:12) We Christians are not to be weak, jelly-backed, wet noodle individuals. I need to look in the mirror while saying that. I know one of the reasons I was caught in a web of deception for so long is because I was one to always avoid confrontation at any cost. "Don't rock the boat was my theme song." Do not make waves. Do not offend. I did not know that I was offending simply by the fact that I was alive because the devil wants to kill, steal and destroy.

Being quiet will not make anything go away. Satan knows that. "Be sober, be vigilant; because your adversary the devil, as a roaring lion, walketh about, seeking whom he may devour."(1 Peter 4:8)

Do not stand quietly and passively by while what is rightfully yours is being torn asunder by the enemy. Soldiers must be trained to fight. They must be prepared to be warriors. You must have courage and love the Lord so much that you are willing to engage in spiritual warfare. When you learn to fight spiritual warfare, the results will be manifested in the natural realm, so put on that Ephesians six armor and go forward.

It is easier to keep a house in order than it is to wait until everything is in disarray and then try to clean it up. After my husband and I joined a church in 1981, I thought things would get better, based upon the fact that we had joined a church together. Oh how misinformed I was. You have to use the authority and the tools God has given you. Acts 2:38 is just the beginning. "Repent and be baptized in the name of Jesus Christ for the remission of sins and you shall receive the Holy Ghost." That passage of scripture goes on to say, "Save your selves from this untoward generation." Untoward means corrupt. If you do not learn how to fight spiritual warfare, you will be consumed and destroyed by the enemy. Corruption does not go away until deliverance comes. That is when the cleansing and healing occurs.

It is essential that you unite with a Bible believing church that is preaching and teaching the Truth. Develop a prayer life and have fellowship with the saints of God. Do not let the devil trick you into being a loner. Forsake not the assembling of yourselves together. There is strength in unity. Run to the Rock. A rock is relentless, persistent, hard, stable, firm, unrelenting, and it does not yield to outside pressure. That Rock is Jesus.

Malachi 3:17 said, "When I make up my jewels, I will spare

them." Whom is God talking about? You, if you are in Christ. If you are not in Christ, come into the ark of safety. What are you waiting for? Allow God to put you into His jewelry box. Malachi 3:16 says a book of remembrance was written before him for them that feared the Lord, and that thought upon His name. Is your name written in the lamb's book of life?

Look girlfriend, I know what it is like to speak and to be ignored. I know what it is like to be tongue-lashed by the same tongue that spoke words from the bible across the pulpit. I know how it feels to be told to "shut up, your opinion doesn't matter". I know the oppression of living in fear and torment. I also know what it is like to be able to call upon the name of the Lord and to commune with God in the wee hours of the morning and tell Him things you would not tell anyone else. I can truly say with authority that God is my help and in Him do I trust. "The name of the Lord is a strong tower. The righteous runneth into it and is safe." (Proverbs 18:10. Bless the Lord that redeemeth my life from destruction (both now and in the hereafter). I will ask again, "Is your name written in the lamb's book of life?"

Memorizing and repeating scriptural affirmations will indeed prepare you for spiritual warfare. You can draw strength from the Word and find direction for your life. If necessary, post them all over your house. Put them on the mirrors in the bathroom and the bedroom. Tape them to the dashboard in your car. Put them in a conspicuous place at your job-site. Quote them to yourself as often as you can.

Sister, believe me when I tell you, you are not alone. I pray that the living, breathing organism called the church, not that dead unproductive organization called the church, will allow Jesus' life-giving blood to flow to every part of the body to nurture, revitalize and heal it. An organism implies life and growth. There is cohesiveness within that body. It is a group of organized believers. Sister if you are a part of that body, be blessed and be healed. Stretch out, and let the blood of Jesus and the Word of God wash and cleanse you. Do not hide your pain. Do not keep it a secret. Tell the truth and shame the devil. Then you may receive help.

For years, I lived a life of deception. I had to repent to God because living a lie is the same as speaking a lie. In the scriptures, the word conversation refers to your lifestyle. I had to ask God to forgive me for honoring a man more than I did Him. I had allowed my husband to become my idol. I was more concerned about pleasing him and making him happy, than I was God. I know we are to care for the things of the world if we are married, but not to the extent that we break God's laws. The Bible gives us scriptures that tell us how to be godly homemakers. See 1 Corinthians the eleventh chapter and Ephesians the fifth chapter.

Everyone thought we lived in holy matrimony, when actually we existed in a deep, dark demonic stronghold. As long as I kept the lie under wraps and kept coming back to it, this allowed me to be controlled, manipulated and used by evil forces. We have to be mature enough to know when we are following the leading of the Holy Spirit, and not the leading of our fleshly desires.

NOTES

Deliverance

O.K. Here is a part you may have to wrestle
with. I am going to be very straightforward and
tell you that I did for a long time. You must forgive! Get rid of the malice, the anger, the bitterness, the pain and resentment. What do you feel
when you see the person that hurt you? What do
you feel when you hear the person's name that
did these things to you? How do you respond
when you are in a conversation regarding that
person? That is not necessarily past tense. Some
of my sisters are still going through. I suffered
in silence for years but I am so glad God was
merciful and longsuffering. He kept me in spite
of the condition of my heart. Remember, He
said, "I will spare them." We have to be certain
we have allowed the Word to cleanse us. James
3:10 tells us "Out of the same mouth proceeded
blessing and cursing. My brethren, these things
ought not so to be."

I stayed in the marriage longer than I should
have because I ended up compromising my in-
tegrity and desecrating the Word of God within
my heart, while living a lie and doing things that

were not pleasing to God. Some would say I was married to an unbeliever after reading this book, but I was married to a man that professed Christianity.

Come to the realization that forgiveness means not holding something against a person; not reliving the situation continually. You must take it out of the loop. Do not keep rehashing it. Give it to Jesus. There is no "but" there, as in "I forgive you, but". We are not to retaliate. Vengeance belongs to the Lord. Pray for those who despitefully use you. That is a bondage breaker if ever there was one. Give up your right to hold it against them. Forgive and move on with your life. Let the Holy Ghost lead and guide you. He cannot do that if you do not have a prayer life and you are not in communication with God.

This is presuming that you are saved according to Act 2:38, "Repent, and be baptized every one of you in the name of Jesus Christ for the remission of sins, and ye shall receive the gift of the Holy Ghost."

Forgiving does not mean you continue to let someone misuse you. When you forgive, you are able to pray for that person and not hold a grudge against them. Do not talk about them in a negative light, as though you are trying to retaliate with your words. Do not try to get back at them or as the world says, "fight fire with fire." At one point in my transition, I seized upon every opportunity to say as many negative things about my husband as I felt someone would listen to. We are to fight fire with prayer. However, forgiving does not mean to tolerate sin.

When I made the decision to leave the strong hold I was

living in, I came to the realization that removing yourself physically does not release you spiritually, emotionally or mentally. I found out real quick that where you treasure is, that is where your heart is. Now I can truly say my treasure and precious possessions are in the Lord Jesus Christ and His kingdom. I forsook clothes, car, house and all my personal belongings for the security, comfort and peace that God offers. For reasons unknown to me, those possessions were withheld from me for a few years. My husband would not allow me to enter the house again to retrieve them. Three years later, after the divorce was finalized, the court mandated for me to retrieve my personal possessions.

At first, I refused to go to man's law. I truly believed the Lord would restore everything. In deed, the Lord has restored. He has restored over and beyond what I expected, and not the way I thought. In March of 2006, I finally received a divorce because I had to separate my name from his for legal and business purposes.

The Lord has blessed me "exceeding abundantly above all" I could ask or think, according to the power that worketh in me. (See Ephesians 3:20) The most precious possession I have acquired is the peace of God that passes all understanding.

There is absolutely nothing to compare to the peace of God that passes all understanding. The natural man cannot comprehend or apprehend what sweet communion and fellowship with God is like. I walked away from all those creature comforts I had accumulated in the past forty-one years. The enemy seems to have thought if he withheld them from me, I would yield to pressure and fall back into the trap he had set for me more than once. I say not so! Jehovah-Jirah is my provider.

I often say that God shows His love for me through the people that He has placed in my life. Some of them have shared their resources in the way of finances, shelter, and fellowship, but most of all prayer.

Now be forewarned, if you ask God to cleanse you, He can be brutally up front and personal. While you are trying to shift the focus to what has been done to you, He will focus on you, period. When there is infection in your body, it will find a way to rid itself of that infection. Your system will send out antibodies to fight the infection. The same principle applies in the spirit realm. The Holy Spirit will war against invading, foreign substances. The Word must be allowed to cleanse you. It is the antibody needed to cleanse you. It will fight the infection that is invading your life through sin. It will build up your spiritual immune system.

Forgiveness and love operate hand in hand. They help stabilize each other. You cannot forgive without God's agape love and you cannot agape love without forgiving. When Jesus makes you free, you will no longer be numb and stagnant, and paralyzed spiritually, while waiting for something to happen. You will make it happen. Your gifts will flow. Your ministry as a servant will open up. You become able to focus on others instead of self. You will feel like you have lost many, many pounds. You will be revitalized, rejuvenated and receive a new zest for life. It is much like a caterpillar turning into a butterfly. You will metamorphose from a dying entity, merely existing, into a vibrant, alive person, full of life.

I now feel like I did when I first received the Holy Ghost on July 6, 1981. My health has improved. My mental attitude and view of life is more exuberant. I realize that some of the symptoms I was experiencing physically were a result of spiritual impairment. "For we wrestle not against flesh and blood, but against principalities, against powers, against the rulers of the darkness of this world, against spiritual wickedness in high places." (Ephesians 6:12)

Honey let me tell you, demonic oppression and bondage are real. It is not a figment of your imagination. People began to tell me they saw more youth and vigor in me, without knowing what they saw was a result of my being delivered. The spiritual experience led to a physical manifestation. I began to live again. Prior to that, I was dead in my trespasses and sins. I was so stressed out. Now I know why stress is considered a silent killer. You are not aware of its creeping paralysis, as it slowly drains life from you.

When your connection to God is opened up, it is better for you than all of the doctor's medicines on this earth. How many times have you heard, "We don't know what the problem is"? Come on saints, we God-fearing people know what the problem is. Physician heal thyself. The church is the hospital operating room. It is where we can come to get the sin cut out.

I am not talking about the edifice called a church. I am referring to the physical/spiritual temple, the body of Christ. If the world comes into the church fellowship for a cure, how can we give that cure if we are too weak and sick ourselves?

Believe me when I tell you that the battle may rage on, but Jesus has already won the war. The battle is not yours. It is the Lord's. Keep in mind that in order to move to the next mountaintop, you have to walk through the valley, but you will not walk alone. I was talking with my Pastor's wife one day, and she said she looks at the valley as being a place of refuge, with greenery, plant life and cool refreshing waters, and the mountaintop as a dry, barren, harsh place that is steep and hard to climb. I had never looked at it that way before, and after talking with some saints, they have not received that revelation either. Many of us see the mountaintop as being at the peak or highest point, representing success or overcoming. One thing is certain, no matter where you are in your walk, the Lord is leading you and goodness and mercy are following you on THE WAY OUT.

I have said quite a bit about forgiveness. The key and most essential thing is to realize that Jesus is the source, not you. We easily talk about forgiving others, but the illusion is that we are looking outward at what is around us and trying to force it into our spirit, instead of allowing the Spirit to work from the inside to the outside.
Forgiveness must be internalized. Jesus sent us the Comforter. He abides within us. We often try to work our problems out from the head instead of the heart.

I did not understand why I was still having nightmares and being attacked by the spirit of oppression, until the Holy Spirit revealed to me that I had not forgiven myself. I was still in bondage. When I gave the burden to the Lord and left it there, I was loosed. I found THE WAY OUT.

Looking Inside
The Jewelry
Box

Open up the jewelry box, so God's precious
jewel can shine forth. The time is at hand. He
is ready to act. This is the season. The Lord will
return to gather his precious jewels. Only those
that have been shaped, cut and polished shall
be among His jewels. Do not be a castaway, a
throwaway, or what Paul referred to as dung.
God loves you and has predestined what kind
of jewel you will be, but only you can determine
the quality.

Please believe me when I tell you, you are precious in His sight. You are His treasured possession. Gemstones come in different sizes, shapes
and colors, but they can all be kept in the same
box.

As you contemplate that thought, you come to
the realization that God's church is supposed

to consist of variety. "After this I beheld, and, lo, a great multitude, which no man could number, of all nations, and kindreds, and people, and tongues, stood before the throne, and before the Lamb, clothed with white robes, and palms in their hands." (Revelation 7:9) The palms represented a victory celebration. We are truly victorious when God brings us out.

When we place our personal jewels in a jewelry box, it is usually lined with a soft velvet or silk material, something that will not be abrasive. Usually a fabric that will cushion and not irritate or scratch the jewelry is used. It protects it from any trauma, distress or damage of any kind. How much more do you think God will protect and shelter those that belong to Him?

In John the fourth chapter, to most of us, the woman at the well may have been perceived as a piece of black coal, but to Jesus, she was a diamond in the making. Jesus sat down at that well to rest. Don't you want Him to sit down and rest where you are? Isn't it wonderful when He meets you at the place where you need Him most? You want that place to be away from listening ears and prying eyes. It is there, where He can minister to you in solitude and prepare you so you can minister to others. The disciples had gone into town to buy food. What does that mean? To me it infers that the church is going on about its "business as usual" but Jesus will be there for you, to minister to you, and to show you your sins. He will heal you and bind up your wounds. He will accept you as you are and give you eternal life.

Be honest with Him. You may be ashamed to tell another

person where you have been. You may be embarrassed or yes, even too proud to let it be known what happened to you, but tell it all to Jesus. I wondered how this book would be received because I had virtually been told to suck it up so many times by well-meaning Christians. I thank God for the realization that the story needed to be told or I would not be released from that strong intimidating spirit of bondage, and there are others that need to hear it in order to be freed. "This is the season for uncovering", was pressed into my spirit, and until I became obedient to that mandate, I knew I would not be released from the spirit of intimidation, until I complied. My main concern and first priority is being obedient to God.

The woman at the well said, "I have no husband." Jesus replied, "Thou hast well said." Then He proceeded to heal her, to meet her needs, and to offer salvation and deliverance. He ministered to her there by the side of that well. He did not tell her she had to go to the temple. He did not tell her she had to join a congregation. He did not tell her she had to perform or do works of any kind. "For by grace are ye saved through faith; and that not of yourselves: it is the gift of God." (Ephesians 2:8). All she had to do was believe. At the end of the story she said, "Is not this the Christ?"

Verse 23 says, "True worshippers shall worship the Father in spirit and in truth. For the Father seeketh such to worship Him. Is He seeking for you? Is He looking for you? Are you a true worshipper? Remember our theme text, in Malachi 3 implies in the NIV, that He is getting ready to act. Something has to happen, in order for the process to be completed. Time is winding up. It is imperative that we get in place. Worship the Lord thy God in spirit and in truth.

John 4:27 says the disciples returned and were surprised to find Him talking to her. Some of the church members will want to know why Mary Blueberry is ushering at the door of God's house, when she used to be on the corner picking up Johns. Some may say Sally Sugar-foot was raped, and molested, is she the right one to be teaching our child in the children's church? In addition, God forbid if the pastor's wife had an abortion before she became a new creature in Christ, how is she going to speak to the missionaries about holiness and purity? Do you see where I am going with this? Some will turn and go the other way when they see you coming. These are the ones who have forgotten what God delivered them from. "Wherefore, as by one man sin entered into the world, and death by sin; and so death passed upon all men, for that all have sinned" (Romans 5:12)

Silence may prevail when you enter a room. Your phone will not ring as often, but that is all right, as long as you are in communion with the Lord. You will find yourself praying more, and reading your Bible more, and that is a good thing. Remember to pray for those that despitefully use you, and there is not a friend like the lowly Jesus.

After Jesus ministered to the woman, she left what she was doing. She left what was being done to her. She moved away from that and began to minister to those who had been in various relationships with her.
They were her abusers, accusers, molesters, desecraters, users and those that had violated her and used her to commit

incest, fornication or whatever. She went into the town and told everybody "Come see a man, which told me all things that ever I did. Is not this the Christ?" She wanted them to share in her newly found liberation from sin. "He sent His Word, and healed them, and delivered them from their destructions." (Psalms 107:20)

Please do not misunderstand me. I cannot say it enough. I am not advocating divorce and/or separation in marriage. It is the first institution God sanctioned. God does not approve of divorce. Because He knows the hearts of men (humankind), He allowed for divorce and separation under certain conditions. Perhaps this is a good subject for your Pastor to teach more on. I am not going to elaborate on doctrinal matters in this book.

Some scriptures to read and to pray for Holy Spirit to open up your understanding about this matter, are Deuteronomy 24:1-4; Matthew 5:31-32; Matthew 19:3-12; Mark 10:2-12; and 1 Corinthians 7:25-40.

I will say that there is nowhere in the Bible that God condones bondage. He allowed the Israelites to go through bondage because of their disobedience. The same principle can apply to divorce. I never agreed to divorce, but my husband divorced me first in 1997 and I remarried him in 1998. As of the writing of this book, we divorced again in 2006. We both filed within the same month in 2003, but for reasons unknown to me, his lawyer withdrew from the case and he did not hire another one after he found the results would not be to his satisfaction, but I stayed with the procedure for legal reasons, until it was completed in March 2006. I am not trying to defend myself. I am allowing the Lord to release my sisters from bondage.

The Lord will free you from bondage. When He does, then it is time to move forward either as a married person or as a single person. No one should be able to tell you, you cannot do a work for the Lord, and that you are scarred for life. Christ took care of that at the cross.

This letter is to my sisters that are in a hard place because you are confused by the legalistic teachings that are binding you. No one has ministered to you and you feel like an outcast.

Hold your head up. Do not worry about your self-esteem, for you are highly esteemed. The Lord is with you. You are blessed among women.

God honors and elevates women who are receptive and open to His spirit. He lifts them up to higher heights and deeper depths in Him. Rahab, the harlot became a descendent of Jesus Christ. Ruth the Moabitess came into the bloodline of Jesus also. Deborah was a homemaker and the Lord used her mightily. When Christ encountered the widow of Nain He was filled with so much compassion for her that He raised her son from the dead. Jesus was so moved with compassion by the sinner woman that washed His feet with her tears, dried them with her hair and anointed them with precious oil, that He memorialized her.

All of us come from various backgrounds but God can be glorified. We are all God's jewels. We are His precious possessions. "For we are His workmanship, created in Christ Jesus unto good works, which God hath before ordained that we should walk in them." (Ephesians 2:10). You may feel like you are in hell right now, but the gates of hell shall not prevail against the church. God has a place for you in His kingdom. He is working on us. He is making up His treasured possessions.

NOTES

_____

_____

_____

_____

_____

_____

_____

_____

Closure

We must stay in the Word so we can know the difference between God working on us and the devil stalking us. There are some things we encounter that we do not have to tolerate, because we have Holy Ghost power. That is why we need a strong prayer life, so we can deflect the fiery darts that are being hurled at us. Always keep your prayer armor on. We must keep the lines of communication open so Holy Ghost can lead and guide us. When we do not know what to pray or how to pray, "Likewise the Spirit also helpeth our infirmities: for we know not what we should pray for as we ought: but the Spirit itself maketh intercession for us with groanings which cannot be uttered." (Romans 8:26)

Do not let the cares of life stop up your lifeline of communication with God. When you are being accosted and confronted from every side, just remember, Jesus is our intercessor. This does not negate your prayer life. You must pray, pray, pray.

Plaque can clog up your veins and stop the

blood from bringing life to the body. The cares of this life can stop the life-giving flow to your spirit. When you have allowed so many things to fill in the places in your spirit where the Word should be, they push the Word out and life is gradually drained from you.

"Now therefore, ye are no more strangers and foreigners, but fellow citizens with the saints, and of the household of God." (Ephesians 2:19). We are His jewels. We are in the jewelry box. While you are being prepared, it is the shepherds' job to feed you. I am referring to your Pastor in this instance. He (or she) has taken on the task of watching over your soul and seeing after your spiritual needs. He will have to give an account for it. He should be able to help you to seek the kingdom first, to lead you in the way of righteousness and to be there when you need Godly counsel, (not every time you do not want the responsibility of making decisions or you are drinking milk instead of eating meat).

Some of us are shortening the lives of our pastor's and their wives with trivial pursuit. I praise God that I have a pastor and first lady that are there for me and lift me up in prayer, and I pray for them also.

I especially want to take a hallelujah break and say something to the single women. Wait on God. Because you are single, it does not mean you are not complete. Single means one unit that is complete within itself. If God so desires to join you with a mate, then you become one with your mate, which also exemplifies completeness or wholeness. While you are waiting on a mate, you are still one. You are a complete unit in Jesus Christ. Oh the omniscience of God!

Seek ye first the Kingdom of God and His righteousness and all these things (your creature comforts, your job promotion, the loneliness removed, a new car, a house, and yes, your husband, if that is what God has ordained for you), will be added unto you. The brother is supposed to look for you. You are not supposed to seek after him.

Do not let others tell you that you have to look a certain way, act a certain way and acquire certain things to be acceptable. Looking a certain way will not make you a part of the body of Christ, but being in the body of Christ, will make you look a certain way. I hope you see the significance there.

You are more than all right when you are resting in the Lord and seeking His will for your life, not trying to emulate Sister Butterfinger's life. Do not seek after the outward adorning, but let your adorning be "the hidden man of the heart, in that which is not corruptible, even the ornament of a meek and quiet spirit, which is in the sight of God of great price." (1 Peter 3:4) Do not be deceived, meekness is not weakness. It is power or strength if you will, under control. It does not suggest that you are to be someone's floor mat to be walked on. As pertaining to godly attire, we must keep a balance. Feel good, look good and smell good without going to extremes.
We are in the world, but we are not of the world. "all that is in the world, the lust of the flesh, and the lust of the eyes, and the pride of life, is not of the Father, but is of the world." (1 John 2:16)

There are many gifts and talents within the body of Christ. Not all of them will operate at the same time or in the same way. God will open His jewelry box and your ministry will flow when it is your season. Everyone has something to contribute.

Just your smile and warm greeting can encourage someone and help him or her make it through another day. Of course if you are a sister encouraging a brother, it must be done decent and in order.

"Neither give place to the devil. Let no corrupt communication proceed out of your mouth, but that which is good to the use of edifying, that it may minister grace unto the hearers." (Ephesians 4:27, 29) A phone call sometimes is needed when you want to encourage someone. Prayer is always appropriate. In some cases, it would not hurt to send a card.

Take it from the voice of experience, if you let the flesh make your decisions in life, you will live to regret it, or should I say die to regret it? Wait on the Lord. "This I say then, walk in the Spirit, and ye shall not fulfill the lust of the flesh." (Galatians 5:16)

I did not know Jesus as my Savior when I met my husband. I was young, naïve and inexperienced. I saw a tall, brown-skinned, good-looking man that showed more interest in me than anyone had ever shown me. I was untouched and untainted as pertaining to worldly things. I took pride in having a husband and living a fairy tale "and they lived happily ever after" life. I wanted to get married and have children. I thought it was my sole purpose in life, as a female.

Young women, avoid the octopus whose hands are everywhere, usually in the wrong places, and the one who can "bend the truth" without batting an eye. Learn to discern. Pray for God to give you wisdom as you walk through this world. Listen to your elders' voice of experience. Many of them have "been there, done that, and won the tee-shirt."

NOTES

_____

_____

_____

_____

_____

_____

_____

_____

I strongly admonish couples to seek counseling with your Pastor before you get married. Most Pastors that I know will not perform a marriage ceremony unless they give counseling to the couple first. Some set a limit of at least three weeks in counseling. That is not enough. I would suggest at least six months with the sessions being held weekly. Most couples are pathetically unprepared for marriage, which is a lifetime commitment. An adequate number of personal meetings are necessary and a class with other betrothed couples is beneficial.

I disregarded the words of wisdom that were offered to me by those near me, who were more experienced in life. I used my five senses:

1. Hearing (smooth words)
2. Sight (tall and good-looking)
3. Taste (He wined and dined me)
4. Touch (I liked the way his touch made me feel)
5. Smell (you can be seduced by the mellow fragrance of the right cologne and/or aftershave.

I was strictly walking in the flesh because I was not saved and did not know anything about walking in the spirit; therefore, I had no spiritual discernment. "But the natural man receiveth not the things of the Spirit of God: for they are foolishness unto him: neither can he know them, because they are spiritually discerned." (1 Corinthians 2:14)

Being saved will prepare you for heaven and it will also prepare you for living. When you are saved and filled with the Holy Ghost, you will seek after the things of God and not the things of the world. You will learn how to align your priorities.

Eat the word. The word is not just for old folks who some say have already lived their lives. Holiness and sanctification is for all believers. Timothy was young and God used him mightily. Mary the mother of Jesus was young, and wow! David was a young lad. Esther was a young woman and God used her to save a whole nation. Being young does not excuse you from living a godly, holy life.

You must know that the attacks of the enemy, incest, molestation, and being abused do not separate you from the love of God. Do not be enticed by the counterfeit offerings put on display by the world. They will crumble and disintegrate around you and leave you destitute and without hope.

There was a song a few years back that said, "I wanna know what love is." I can answer that for you. God is love. Seek after God, find God and do not let go of Him.

You are God's jewel; His treasured possession. I know Howard the coward thought you were a punching bag. Separate yourself and do not go back to that. I know that man told you if you loved him you would do whatever he asks, including fornication, adultery, perversion, drugs, alcohol, lying, stealing and anything else the devil can throw at you. He has your number. Do not listen to his lies any longer. You have to love God and yourself first and then you will learn to love others with God's agape love.

Please, please, please get acquainted with the person you

are intending to marry. Talk and ask questions. Do not leave any stone unturned. Find out about his upbringing. What was his childhood like? What are his likes and dislikes? IS HE SAVED? Is the fruit of the Spirit growing? What are his short-term and long-term goals? What about children? What is his outlook on discipline? What are his thoughts on finances, housing and other things relating to the stability of the family? You cannot ask too many questions. There are many other areas of life I could mention but the main idea is to get to know with whom you want to share the rest of your life. What is in it (marriage) for you? What will the consequences be? What are your expectations? Look at both sides of the coin to see if they correspond or match. Do you agree on the vital life altering issues of life?

Allow God to clean you up and fix you up. Do not be like the pig that goes back to the mud. You know the pieces you bought from Wal-Mart are made from something that shines and looks like gold or silver and are low-maintenance. Those expensive precious pieces that you bought from Saks Fifth Avenue and Nieman-Marcus are made from the real stuff and have to receive special care. They will last a lifetime. They need to be buffed and polished sometimes. The setting has to be tightened from time to time. What am I saying? Do you want to be ordinary, everyday; run of the mill, common costume jewelry or do you want to be an especially treasured possession? Become one of God's jewels. Allow Him to prepare you for life.

Will you be ready when God returns to make up His jewels? Do you belong to Him? Whom are you serving? Are you His treasured possession? Do not fall between the cracks on THE WAY OUT. God will put you in His jewelry box to hold you, protect you and secure you. Let the Holy Ghost lead and guide you.

When it is time for you to leave that situation you are in be sure you have committed yourself to fasting and praying. The Holy Ghost will tell you where to go or whom to go to for help. Not everyone is prepared to assist you. More churches need "safe places". There needs to be a place where women can go for godly counsel and assistance. Some people do not think they need counseling. Read Psalms 1 to see what God says about counseling.

Earlier, I commented on collecting offering. It takes money to run a ministry. Many churchgoers are not willing to support the ministries of the church with their money or their time. Those Levites assigned to collecting the offerings should not have to beg. Uncle Sam takes his right off the top but God wants you to be a cheerful giver. Be grateful that you have something to give. It all belongs to God, yet we do not want to freely give as we have freely received. I have heard some, have the audacity to verbalize, that they will not give money to the preacher. You are not giving it to the preacher. You are giving to the work of God for Kingdom building. "For the scripture saith, Thou shalt not muzzle the ox that treadeth out the corn. And, The labourer is worthy of his reward."(1 Timothy 5:18)

After we pray for people, we must help take care of their natural needs if necessary or their spiritual needs will succumb to the cares of the world. This is where the real ministering takes place. What better way is there to serve people than to help meet their needs? "If a brother or sister be naked, and destitute of daily food, And one of you say unto them, Depart in peace, be ye warmed and filled; notwithstanding ye give them not those things which are needful to the body; what doth it profit?" (James 2:15-16). Yes, God will provide through the body of believers called the church. If the finances are not there, through the giving of tithes and offerings, the church cannot function as it was designed to do. The electric company and other utility companies do not give churches a break. The bills have to be paid the same as in your home. The Pastor has to support his family and put gas in his car, the same as you.

God has placed resources within the body of Christ that can help us resolve many of the issues that confront us daily. We must seek and expect God to be our main resource. We must be connected to the power. "Study to show thyself approved unto God, a workman that needeth not to be ashamed, rightly dividing the word of truth." (1 Timothy 2:15) If we want the light to come on, we have to flip the switch. Use what is readily available to you. Walk in the Spirit, not in the flesh.

We need someone within our congregations that can minister to those of us that have been infected by incest, molestation and/or abuse. Yes, I used the word infected instead of affected, because those types of conditions can lead to devastating results. We can become contaminated, defiled, damaged, polluted or perhaps destroyed.

Computers have the capability to perform a preventive maintenance procedure called defragmenting. This procedure helps to prevent the loss of items stored on the hard drive. With regular defragmenting, the life of the hard drive is extended. During this process, the hard disk is scanned for errors and unnecessary files. So it is with our spiritual health, we should defragment often. Get rid of all the unnecessary garbage and nonessential things that can harm us. Our performance or presentation is optimized. We are made the better for it in all phases of our life.

It is time out for hoping it will go away if you do not talk about it or pretend it is not there. The laws are structured in a way now that does not allow pastors to legally counsel unless they are a "licensed Christian counselor". That is a ministry within itself. People are looking for answers from God and His ministers are His mouthpiece. Malpractice suits are popping up right and left. The world is trying to hinder them in the thing that God has called them to do, but "The gates of hell shall not prevail against the church." (Matthew 16:18)

For years I felt I would betray a trust if I spoke out. I do not know why I felt this way, because we all know the devil comes to kill, steal and destroy. Because I did not speak out, guilt was heaped upon my head and I sank deeper and deeper into bondage. Go to your pastor and/or first lady if you are not comfortable talking to a male about your situation. Through prayer and wise counseling, you will be freed to talk to your pastor. I know there have been people in the pulpit that have abused and misused their authority. You must discern what type of person you are allowing to feed your spirit. If you cannot trust him or her, should you be in that congregation?

There is therefore no condemnation to them that are in Christ Jesus. Do not continue to let the enemy hold you captive. You are not alone. We are all in God's jewelry box and Jesus is THE WAY OUT.

2 Corinthians 1:3-4 says ,"Blessed be God, even the Father of our Lord Jesus Christ, the Father of mercies, and the God of all comfort; Who comforteth us in all our tribulation, that we may be able to comfort them which are in any trouble, by the comfort wherewith we ourselves are comforted of God."

FIND THE WAY OUT! "I SHALL NOT DIE, BUT LIVE AND DECLARE THE WORKS OF THE LORD." (Psalms 118:17)

Your Personal Testimony

Local Resources For Help

Reformed Theological Seminary:
(fee based on income)

Center For Marriage and Family Therapy Counseling
5422 Clinton Boulevard
Jackson, Ms.
601-923-1645

Shelter For Battered Families
601-366-0222
601-366-0757
601-273-9012

Mississippi Coalition Against Dometstic Violence
P.O. Box 4703
Jackson, MS 39296
800-898-3234 (toll free)
601-981-9196
601-982-7372 (fax)

Christians In Action
601- 353-1942

Family Crises Shelter
601-355-3070

Abuse Hotline
1-800-222-8000

Look through your local telephone directory for similar agencies in your area, or seek recommendations from another source.

Biography

Evangelist Voncele Savage is a retired public school teacher, who is presently teaching and encouraging others from the Word of God. She is a member of Parkway Pentecostal Church in Madison, Mississippi. She resides in Canton, Mississippi. Her burden is for women in the church, that need spiritual healing, as a consequence of being in dysfunctional relationships. She is available for conferences, missionary services and other services.

You may contact her at:
voncelekirkwood@bellsouth.net
(601) 859-6938 or (601) 942-0509